Lecture Notes in Computer Science   11519

Commenced Publication in 1973
Founding and Former Series Editors:
Gerhard Goos, Juris Hartmanis, and Jan van Leeuwen

More information about this series at http://www.springer.com/series/7409

Valerie Issarny · Balaji Palanisamy ·
Liang-Jie Zhang (Eds.)

Internet of Things –
ICIOT 2019

4th International Conference
Held as Part of the Services Conference Federation, SCF 2019
San Diego, CA, USA, June 25–30, 2019
Proceedings

Springer

Editors
Valerie Issarny
Inria de Paris
Paris Cedex 12, France

Balaji Palanisamy
University of Pittsburgh
Pittsburgh, PA, USA

Liang-Jie Zhang ⓘ
Kingdee International
Software Group Co., Ltd.
Shenzhen, China

ISSN 0302-9743   ISSN 1611-3349   (electronic)
Lecture Notes in Computer Science
ISBN 978-3-030-23356-3   ISBN 978-3-030-23357-0   (eBook)
https://doi.org/10.1007/978-3-030-23357-0

LNCS Sublibrary: SL3 – Information Systems and Applications, incl. Internet/Web, and HCI

This Springer imprint is published by the registered company Springer Nature Switzerland AG
The registered company address is: Gewerbestrasse 11, 6330 Cham, Switzerland

Preface

With the rapid advancements of mobile Internet, cloud computing and big data, device-centric traditional Internet of Things (IoT) is now moving into a new era, which is termed the "Internet of Things Services" (IOTS). In this era, sensors and other types of sensing devices, wired and wireless networks, platforms and tools, data processing/visualization/analysis and integration engines, and other components of traditional IoT are interconnected through innovative services to realize the value of connected things, people, and virtual Internet spaces. The way of building new IoT applications is changing. We indeed need creative thinking, long-term visions, and innovative methodologies to respond to such a change. The ICIOT 2019 conference was organized to continue to promote research and application innovations around the world.

ICIOT 2019 was part of the Services Conference Federation (SCF). SCF 2019 had the following ten collocated service-oriented sister conferences: 2019 International Conference on Web Services (ICWS 2019), 2019 International Conference on Cloud Computing (CLOUD 2019), 2019 International Conference on Services Computing (SCC 2019), 2019 International Congress on Big Data (BigData 2019), 2019 International Conference on AI & Mobile Services (AIMS 2019), 2019 World Congress on Services (SERVICES 2019), 2019 International Congress on Internet of Things (ICIOT 2019), 2019 International Conference on Cognitive Computing (ICCC 2019), 2019 International Conference on Edge Computing (EDGE 2019), and 2019 International Conference on Blockchain (ICBC 2019). As the founding member of SCF, the First International Conference on Web Services (ICWS) was held in June 2003 in Las Vegas, USA. The First International Conference on Web Services—Europe 2003 (ICWS-Europe 2003) was held in Germany in October 2003. ICWS-Europe 2003 was an extended event of the 2003 International Conference on Web Services (ICWS 2003) in Europe. In 2004, ICWS-Europe was changed to the European Conference on Web Services (ECOWS), which was held in Erfurt, Germany. To celebrate its 16th birthday, SCF 2018 was held successfully in Seattle, USA.

This volume presents the accepted papers for the 2019 International Conference on Internet of Things (ICIOT 2019), held in San Diego, USA, during June 25–30, 2019. For this conference, we accepted 11 papers, including eight full papers and three short papers. Each was reviewed and selected by at least three independent members of the ICIOT 2019 international Program Committee.

We are pleased to thank the authors, whose submissions and participation made this conference possible. We also want to express our thanks to the Organizing Committee and Program Committee members, for their dedication in helping to organize the conference and in reviewing the submissions. We would like to thank Samee U. Khan, who provided continuous support for this conference. We look forward to your great contributions as a volunteer, author, and conference participant for the fast-growing worldwide services innovations community.

May 2019

Valerie Issarny
Balaji Palanisamy
Liang-Jie Zhang

Organization

General Chair

Samee U. Khan National Science Foundation, USA

Program Chairs

Valerie Issarny Inria, France
Balaji Palanisamy University of Pittsburgh, USA

Services Conference Federation (SCF 2019)

General Chairs

Calton Pu Georgia Tech, USA
Wu Chou Essenlix Corporation, USA
Ali Arsanjani 8x8 Cloud Communications, USA

Program Chair

Liang-Jie Zhang Kingdee International Software Group Co., Ltd., China

Finance Chair

Min Luo Services Society, USA

Industry Exhibit and International Affairs Chair

Zhixiong Chen Mercy College, USA

Operations Committee

Huan Chen Kingdee International Software Group Co., Ltd., China
Jing Zeng Kingdee International Software Group Co., Ltd., China
Liping Deng Kingdee International Software Group Co., Ltd., China
Yishuang Ning Tsinghua University, China
Sheng He Tsinghua University, China

Steering Committee

Calton Pu (Co-chair) Georgia Tech, USA
Liang-Jie Zhang (Co-chair) Kingdee International Software Group Co., Ltd., China

ICIOT 2019 Program Committee

Amel Bennaceur	The Open University, UK
Georgios Bouloukakis	University of California, Irvine, CA, USA
Luca Cagliero	Politecnico di Torino, Italy
Tao Chen	University of Birmingham, UK
Siobhán Clarke	Trinity College Dublin, Ireland
Alfredo Goldman	USP, Brazil
Atishay Jain	Adobe Systems, USA
Nagarajan Kandasamy	Drexel University, USA
Ajay Kattepur	TCS Research, India
Shaochun Li	IBM Research (China), China
Yutao Ma	Wuhan University, China
Mirco Musolesi	University College London, UK
Rui André Oliveira	University of Lisbon, Portugal
Françoise Sailhan	CNAM, France
Ashish Tanwer	Stony Brook University, USA
Marisol Garcia Valls	UC3 Madrid, Spain
Nalini Venkatasubramanian	University of California, Irvine, CA, USA
Jian Wang	Wuhan University, China

Contents

Underground Environment Aware MIMO Design Using Transmit and Receive Beamforming in Internet of Underground Things

Abdul Salam[✉]

Department of Computer and Information Technology,
Purdue University, West Lafayette, USA
salama@purdue.edu

Abstract. In underground (UG) multiple-input and multiple-output (MIMO), the transmit beamforming is used to focus energy in the desired direction. There are three different paths in the underground soil medium through which the waves propagates to reach at the receiver. When the UG receiver receives a desired data stream only from the desired path, then the UG MIMO channel becomes three path (lateral, direct, and reflected) interference channel. Accordingly, the capacity region of the UG MIMO three path interference channel and degrees of freedom (multiplexing gain of this MIMO channel requires careful modeling). Therefore, expressions are required derived the degrees of freedom of the UG MIMO interference channel. The underground receiver needs to perfectly cancel the interference from the three different components of the EM-waves propagating in the soil medium. This concept is based upon reducing the interference the undesired components to minimum at UG receiver using the receive beamforming. In this paper, underground environment aware MIMO using transmit and receive beamforming has been developed. The optimal transmit beamforming and receive combining vectors under minimal inter-component interference constraint are derived. It is shown that UG MIMO performs best when all three component of the wireless UG channel are leveraged for beamforming. The environment aware UG MIMO technique leads to three-fold performance improvements and paves the wave for design and development of next generation sensor-guided irrigation systems in the field of digital agriculture.

Keywords: Digital agriculture · Wireless underground channel ·
Underground communications · MIMO · Beamforming ·
Internet of Underground Things

1 Introduction

Internet of Underground Things (IOUT) have many applications in precision agriculture [1,2,5,8,10–12,14–25,29,34–36]. Border monitoring is another

© Springer Nature Switzerland AG 2019
V. Issarny et al. (Eds.): ICIOT 2019, LNCS 11519, pp. 1–15, 2019.
https://doi.org/10.1007/978-3-030-23357-0_1

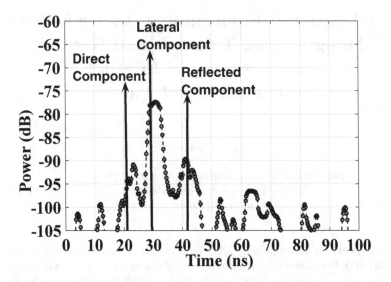

Fig. 1. An example power delay profile (PDP) of the impulse response model of the wireless UG channel [28].

important application area of IOUT, where these networks are being used to enforce border and stop infiltration [3,32]. Monitoring applications of IOUT include land slide monitoring, and pipeline monitoring [10,30,31,33]. IOUT provides seamless access of information collected from agricultural fields through the Internet. IOUT include in situ soil sensing capabilities (e.g., soil moisture, temperature, salinity), and provide the ability to communicate through plants and soil, and real-time information about the environment (e.g., wind, rain, solar). When interconnected with existing machinery on the field (seeders, irrigation systems, combines), IOUT enable complete autonomy on the field, and pave the way for more efficient food production solutions. At agricultural farm level, IOUTs are being used to provide valuable information to the farmers.

UG transmit beamforming using phased array antennas at the transmitter [26] has been used in the underground (UG) communications to maximize the lateral wave [28] by transmitting energy at a particular angle. By using this approach, the energy wastage by sending signals in isotropic direction is reduced by forming the narrow-width beam and steering it accordingly. In underground wireless communications, the aim is to enhance the received signal strength and reduce the interference at the receiver. In over the air (OTA) wireless communications, a strong signal strength is attained by transmitting the signal from multiple antennas by different amplitudes and phases. Through this approach, the received signal components add coherently at the receiver. However, in underground communication due to different wave propagation speed in different communication mediums (e.g., soil and air), coherent combining at the receiver in a constructive manner can not be achieved. Therefore, an environment aware UG multiple-input and multiple-output (MIMO) design is required.

The line-of-sight (LoS) component between the UG transmitter and receiver has limitations because of the higher attenuation in the soil medium. An example power delay profile (PDP) of wireless UG channel is shown in Fig. 1. Moreover, the direct path has shorter range and can not be used to reach at longer distances in the underground medium. Therefore, combined transmit and receive beamforming needs developed using non-LoS components (e.g., lateral and reflected). Since, multipath underground channel well-known [28] and has been studied and empirically validated, UG MIMO can be developed for high data rate and log range communications. In this work, techniques have been developed to maximize the signal strength and minimizing the interference at the receiver. Moreover, UG MIMO beamforming expressions have been developed to maximize the capacity of the underground communications.

The rest of the paper is organized as follows: the background and major contributions of this work are discussed in Sect. 2. The UG MIMO is modeled in Sect. 3. Performance evaluations are done in Sect. 4. The article concludes in Sect. 5.

2   Contributions of This Work

This is the first work to design a fully UG MIMO for the UG communications. The transmit and receive beamforming techniques are considered which communicate through the soil by using UG channel medium. Based on the receiver position, EM waves either travel completely through soil for UG communications or some part of it goes through the air for aboveground (AG) communications.

We leverage an UG channel impulse response model for UG beamforming perspective and identify the major EM wave components. Challenges in UG beamforming are highlighted and use of UG MIMO is motivated. We present the effects of different soil properties on beamforming vectors of the transmitter and receiver. This proposed mechanism estimates the best beam steering angle based on the soil moisture sensing.

We have considered an UG MIMO transceiver system where both transmitter and receiver has the beamforming capability. Additionally, this approach removes the inter-component interference and enhance the received signal strength. Underground environment aware MIMO using transmit and receive beamforming is vital to increased spectral efficiency, enhance communication range, and energy efficiency in next-generation wireless underground networks, which are expected to include underground antenna arrays [26]. UG MIMO approach has potential applications in many practical scenarios such as precision agriculture, ground penetrating radars (GPR), hazardous object search, locating IEDs, transmission structures under the runways for aircraft communications, antennas for geographic research, communications from marshes, geology, and wireless underground sensor networks (WUSNs).

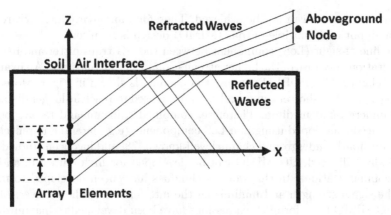

(a) Transmit Beamforming

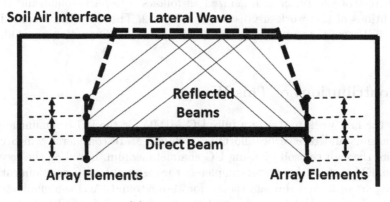

(b) Receive Beamforming

Fig. 2. The communications schematic for UG MIMO.

3 The UG MIMO System Models

The underground nodes communicate with other underground nodes (UG2UG link) and above ground nodes (UG2AG link). Communications schematic for UG MIMO communications is shown in Fig. 2. These aboveground nodes are fixed sinks and mobile nodes mounted on movable infrastructures such as center pivot. In aboveground communications, waves propagating to receiver nodes are refracted from soil-air interface, whereas in UG communications, lateral waves need to be utilized. Desired beam patterns for both scenarios are shown in Fig. 2. In Fig. 2(a), that refractions and reflections of EM waves from the soil-air interface effect the beam patterns propagating to the above-ground node.

In UG MIMO, transmit beamforming [26] is used to focus energy in the desired direction, there are three different paths [28] in the underground soil medium through which the waves propagates to reach at the receiver. When the UG receiver receives a desired data stream only from the desired path, then the UG MIMO channel becomes three path (lateral, direct, and reflected) interference channel. Accordingly, the capacity region of the UG MIMO three path interference channel and degrees of freedom (multiplexing gain of this MIMO channel requires careful modeling). Therefore, expressions are required derived the degrees of freedom of the UG MIMO interference channel.

The underground receiver needs to perfectly cancel the interference from the three different components of the EM-waves propagating in the soil medium. in UG transmit beamforming, limited number of antenna can only achieve low spatial directivity, that leads to presence of signals in undesired direction that cause interference at the receiver. This UG MIMO concept is based upon reducing the interference the undesired components to minimum at UG receiver using the receive beamforming. In this paper, underground environment aware MIMO using transmit and receive beamforming has been developed. The optimal transmit beamforming and receive combining vectors under minimal inter-component interference constraint are derived. Accordingly, UG MIMO techniques are designed and investigated in the underground soil medium. Next we present the system model:

We consider an UG MIMO transceiver system where both transmitter and receiver has the beamforming capability. We also consider that the transmitter node is equipped with two or more transmit antennas and has the beam steering capacity. The receiver node is also equipped with multiple antennas and can receive all three components propagating through underground medium. In this paper, we also assume that the UG MIMO receiver has path selection and switching capability through a selection mechanism which is based on the strength of the received paths at the receiver. Throughout the development of this approach, we also assume equal power allocation at the UG MIMO transmitter. To analyze the achievable capacity using environment aware MIMO using transmit and receive beamforming, we also assume a total power constraint.

Next, we present a zero forcing (ZF) UG MIMO transceiver technique. This approach does not requires the availability of the channel state at the receiver in contrast to the OTA MIMO techniques. Additionally, this approach removes the inter-component interference and enhance the received signal strength. The channel between the underground transmitter T and underground receiver R is represented by $\mathbf{TR}$ of size $N_t \times N_r$ with complex values, where N_t and N_r represents the number of transmit and receive antennas, respectively. The k spatial underground components are distinguished using the $w_1, \ldots, w_k$ where w is associated with component. A $N_t \times N_r$ matrix $\mathbf{I_k}$ denotes the interference between different components. The received signal at the underground receiver by using equal power constraint is given by [6]:

$$y_k = \mathbf{w}_k^* \, \mathbf{TR} \, \mathbf{f}_k \, x_k + \mathbf{w}_k^* \, \mathbf{I}_k \, \mathbf{f}_i \, x_i + \mathbf{w}_k^* \, n_k \tag{1}$$

where x_k is the transmitted signal of the UG component k, and w_k and f_k are the transmit and receive beamforming vectors, n_k is additive white Gaussian noise (AWGN) vector.

Next, we present the expression to maximize the capacity for the low SNR case. From the (1), the received SINR at the UG receiver at the kth component can be expressed as:

$$SINR_k = \frac{\mathbf{w}_k \; \mathbf{f}_k \; \mathbf{f}_k * \mathbf{TR} \; \mathbf{TR}^* \; \mathbf{w}_k^*}{\mathbf{w}_k^*(\mathbf{I}_k \; \mathbf{I}_k * \; \mathbf{f}_i \; \mathbf{f}_i^*)\mathbf{w}_k^*} \tag{2}$$

The achievable capacity for the three underground EM components is defined as:

$$C = \sum_{k=1}^{3} \log_2(1 + SINR_k) \tag{3}$$

Since the objective of this approach is to enhance the channel gain and to remove the inter-component interference, we have only considered the beamforming vectors under the lower bound of achievable capacity. Therefore, maximum rate is not achieved because only the product achievable rate is utilized. Next we present the approach to completely remove the inter-component interference. The instantaneous SNR for every sensed component can be defined as follows when the receive beamforming is not employed at [27]:

$$\gamma_i = \frac{E_b|h_i|^2}{N_0}, \tag{4}$$

where i represents the L, D, or R components. The E_b is the energy per bit and the $|h_i|$ denotes the impulse response.

A three fold increase in SNR (in comparison to a single antenna match filter based design) can be achieved by employing the maximum ratio combining (MRC) approach [13, 27]:

$$\gamma = \sum_{i=1}^{3} w_i \frac{E_b|h_i|^2}{N_0}, \tag{5}$$

where w_i is the weighting factor used for combining. Although SISO approach can be used to maximize the gain, but the reflected components still cause some interference. Therefore, in order to eliminate the undesired interference, the UG MIMO uses transmit beamforming vectors. Accordingly, the received signal can be expressed as [6]:

$$y_k = \mathbf{w}_k^* \; \mathbf{TR} \; \mathbf{f}_k \; x_k + \mathbf{w}_k^* \; \mathbf{I}_k \; \mathbf{f}_i \; x_i + \mathbf{w}_k^* \; n_k \tag{6}$$

$$y_k = \frac{\mathbf{w}_k^* \; \mathbf{TR} \; \mathbf{f}_k \; x_k}{\|\mathbf{TR} \; \mathbf{f}_i\|} + \frac{\mathbf{w}_k^* \; \mathbf{I}_k \; \mathbf{f}_i \; x_i}{\|\mathbf{TR} \; \mathbf{f}_i\|} + \frac{\mathbf{w}_k^* \; n_k}{\|\mathbf{TR} \; \mathbf{f}_i\|} \tag{7}$$

To completely eliminate the interference from (7), MRC approach should satisfy following:

$$\mathbf{w}_1^* \; \mathbf{I}_1 f_i = 0 \tag{8}$$

that can be satisfied by using the transmit beamforming vector. Using this zero interference constraint, MRC beamforming vectors are generalized eigenvectors.

In addition to environment aware weights of UG MIMO, which are based on soil moisture sensing, feedback signals are used to adjust the weights by using the array gain feedback loops. This problem is formulated as maximizing the array gain by using the pilot signals. In this method, UG MIMO array at the transmitter receives the pilot signal in receive mode and then accordingly adjusts its parameters for the transmit mode. In receive mode at the transmitter, scan angles are varied to get the estimate of channel state. The best SNR statistics are used and with change in soil moisture, parameters are adjusted accordingly.

For an array of identical elements, the far-field power density is expressed as [9]:

$$P_{den} = \frac{|E(\theta, \phi)|^2}{120\pi}, \tag{9}$$

where $E(\theta, \phi)$ is the electric filed intensity of the individual array element and is given as:

$$|E(\theta, \phi)| = \sqrt{P_{et}}\sqrt{G_{et}}\frac{\sqrt{30}}{d}, \tag{10}$$

where P_{et}, G_{et} are element transmit power and gain, respectively, and d is the distance. E-field contributions (E_a) from all elements are added together to calculate the array gain G_a [9]. Therefore,

$$G_a(\theta, \phi) = \frac{d^2}{30}\frac{|E_a \varsigma(\theta, \phi)|^2}{P_t}, \tag{11}$$

where ς is the element phase factor and

$$E_a = \frac{\sqrt{30}}{d}\sum_n \sqrt{P_{et}}\sqrt{G_{et}}. \tag{12}$$

The received power at the receiver is presented next. Effective isotropic radiated power (EIRP) can be expressed as product of the transmitted power and antenna gain:

$$P_{rad} = G_t P_t, \tag{13}$$

where P_t is the transmitted power and G_t is the array gain.

The far-field power density P_{av} can is expressed as [7]:

$$P_{av} = P_{av}^D + P_{av}^R + P_{av}^L. \tag{14}$$

where D, R, L denotes the power densities of the direct, reflected and lateral component [28]. The received power is calculated as the product of far-field power density P_{av} and antenna aperture $(\lambda_s^2/4\pi)$. The received power is given as [7]:

$$
\begin{aligned}
P_r^d &= P_t + 20\log_{10}\lambda_s - 20\log_{10}r_1 - 8.69\alpha_s r_1 \\
&\quad -22 + 10\log_{10}D_{rl}, \\
P_r^r &= P_t + 20\log_{10}\lambda_s - 20\log_{10}r_2 - 8.69\alpha_s r_2 \\
&\quad +20\log_{10}\Gamma - 22 + 10\log_{10}D_{rl}, \\
P_r^L &= P_t + 20\log_{10}\lambda_s - 40\log_{10}d - 8.69\alpha_s(h_t + h_r) \\
&\quad +20\log_{10}T - 22 + 10\log_{10}D_{rl},
\end{aligned} \tag{15}
$$

where Γ and T are reflection and transmission coefficients [7], and λ_s is the wavelength in soil. The received power, for an isotropic antenna, is expressed as [7]:

$$P_r = 10 \log_{10}(10^{\frac{P_r^d}{10}} + 10^{\frac{P_r^r}{10}} + 10^{\frac{P_r^L}{10}}). \qquad (16)$$

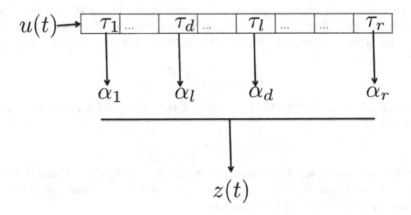

Fig. 3. A realization of the UG channel model with three components.

4   Performance Analysis

In this section, we present the performance analysis of the UG MIMO. First, the model evaluations and results of the transmit beamforming are presented in the next section.

4.1   Transmit Beamforming

To evaluate the developed scheme, we consider the transmit MMSE, ZFBF, and MRT beamforming of [4]. The implementation of the heuristic beamforming schemes (MRT, ZFBF, transmit MMSE/regularized ZFBF/SLNR-MAX beamforming, and the corresponding power allocation) is also based on the [4]. For the UG MIMO application, instead of randomly generating OTA channels, we use the UG channel impulse response [28], where root mean square (RMS) delay spread, distribution of the RMS delay spread, mean amplitude across multiple profiles for a fixed T-R displacement, effects of soil moisture on peak amplitudes of power delay profiles, mean access delay, and coherence bandwidth statistics are presented based on the measured data collected from UG channel experiments. A realization of the UG channel model is shown in Fig. 3. It is important to note here that the calculation of optimal beamforming is not performed in this work because of its computational complexity. The range of the considered SNR values is $-10\,\text{dB}$ to $30\,\text{dB}$.

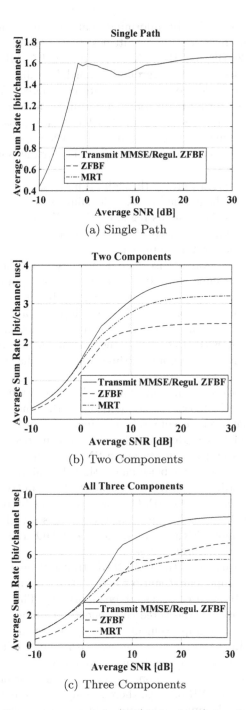

(a) Single Path

(b) Two Components

(c) Three Components

Fig. 4. UG MIMO: the average sum rate (bit/channel use) as a function of change in average SNR.

For the simulations, the beamforming matrices are generated for sum rates with different beamforming strategies (e.g., MRT, ZFBF, transmit MMSE/regularized ZFBF/SLNR-MAX). Accordingly, UG MIMO evaluation is done for different paths of the underground channel. The direct, lateral, and the reflected paths of the underground channel are considered. After the channel matrices are generated for all realizations, accordingly, for each realization normalized beamforming matrices are computed for each approach. Furthermore, by using the branch-reduce-and-bound (BRB) algorithm, based on the proposed approach, pre-allocate matrix serves as the feasible starting points for the BRB algorithm.

Accordingly, the system iterates through all powers. Due to its dependency on the transmit power, the normalized beamforming vectors for transmit MMSE beamforming (which is the same as regularized ZFBF and SLNR-MAX beamforming) are also computed similarly. The sum rate is calculated accordingly for the three different beamforming approaches.

Next, we present the evaluations done using these beamforming approaches for the three different components. In Fig. 4, the average sum rate (bit/channel use) is shown as a function of change in average SNR. The case in which only the single (direct) element is considered is shown in Fig. 4(a). It can be observed that the average sum rate range is 1.5 to 1.7 and it does not change significantly with change in average SNR. Because, in the case of single component, there is no beamforming involved. Therefore, all three approaches have the same average sum rate.

In Fig. 4(b), the average sum rate for the direct and reflected components (two component case) is shown. In comparison to the single path scenario, it can be observed that average sum rate has increased from 1.6 to 3.1 at the average SNR value of 10 dB. Moreover, for the two component case, it can also be observed that the at the lower average SNR of 0 dB, there is only minor difference of 0.1 average sum rate between the three beamforming approaches. At the average SNR of 10 dB, the difference between ZFBF and MMSE is increased to 0.7, which shows that the UG MIMO approach has the better performance as compared to the ZFBF. This difference further increases with increase in SNR which shows that in higher SNR regimes, the UG MIMO transmission approach leads to even improved performance gain.

This better performance of the UG MIMO transmit beamforming improves further in the three component scenario where all three components (e.g., direct, lateral, and reflected) are used transmit beamforming. This scenario has been shown in Fig. 4(c). Overall, the three components beamforming scenario leads to significant performance improvements as compared to the two path transmit beamforming case. In comparison to the two path scenario, it can be observed that average sum rate has increased from 3.1 to 6.6 at the average SNR value of 10 dB. Moreover, for the three component case, it can also be observed that even the at the lower average SNR of 0 dB, there are minor difference of average sum rate between the three beamforming approaches. At the average SNR of 10 dB, the difference between ZFBF and MMSE is increased to 2.7. It is also interesting to note that at the average SNR of 30 dB, the average sum rate reached at the maximum value of 8.4 which shows that the UG MIMO approach performs best when all three components are used for underground transmit beamforming.

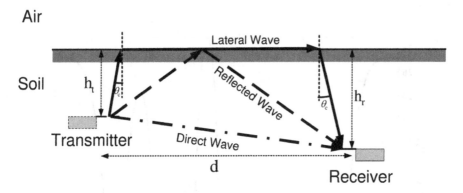

Fig. 5. The direct, reflected, and lateral waves in the underground channel [28].

4.2   Receive Beamforming

For the receive beamforming of the UG MIMO, a 16-element uniform linear array with inter-element distance of half wavelength is used. The operation frequency of 300 MHz is employed. In underground communications, a higher path loss is observed at higher frequencies [28]. The soil has higher permittivity as compared to the air, which leads to the wavelength shortening. Due to the soil permittivity factor, frequency bands in lower spectrum are more suitable for long range communications. Moreover, distance, depth, and soil water content also affects the path loss in underground communications, which requires environment-aware operation frequency selection.

We consider the reception of the received signal through the UG MIMO receive beamforming. In UG communications, there are three main components (e.g. direct, lateral, and reflected (see Fig. 5). The received signal that originates from 10°–15° azimuth has the highest received power. The UG channel has excess delays extending up to 100 ns and root mean square (RMS) delay spread values up to 50 ns. The attenuation varies over 50 dB dynamic range. The direct wave (second received signal) is received from 90° azimuth (direct path, line-of-sight component). It is also known that arrival time of multipath components follows lateral wave based 3-wave UG channel model such that the direct wave reaches at the receiver first before the lateral and reflected components for shorter communication distances [28]. The third wave (the reflected signal) travels towards to the soil-air interface and reaches at the receiver from 45° azimuth. Its total path is also completely through the soil.

The three received signals at the UG MIMO receiver are not correlated with each other and can be distinguished because of different propagation speed in the stratified soil medium. This leads to different inter-element delays that assist different these elements in time. The uniform white noise is considered across all array elements. A beam-scan spatial spectrum estimator is used based on the arrival directions of these three components of the underground channel impulse response.

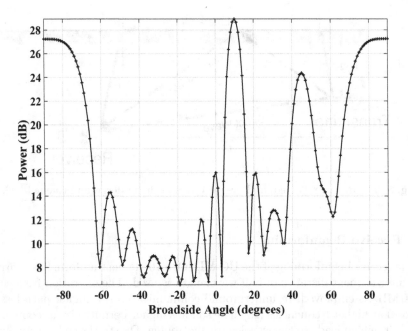

Fig. 6. The spatial spectrum of the three components of the UG MIMO receive beamforming.

In Fig. 6, the spatial spectrum of the three components in the UG MIMO receive beamforming is shown. The plot shows a high power gains at 10° which corresponds to the lateral wave. The lower power gain is exhibited at the 90°, which represents the direct wave. The lower peak at the 45° indicates the reflected wave that due to the lower path in the soil has the lowest gain.

5   Conclusions

In this paper, an UG MIMO technique is developed for transmit and receive beamforming in the underground soil medium. The optimal transmit beamforming and receive combining vectors under minimal inter-component interference constraint are derived. It is shown that UG MIMO performs best when all three component of the wireless UG channel are leveraged for beamforming. The environment aware UG MIMO technique leads to three-fold performance improvements and paves the wave for design and development of next generation sensor-guided irrigation systems in the field of digital agriculture.

References

1. Abrudan, T.E., Kypris, O., Trigoni, N., Markham, A.: Impact of rocks and minerals on underground magneto-inductive communication and localization. IEEE Access **4**, 3999–4010 (2016)
2. Akyildiz, I.F., Stuntebeck, E.P.: Wireless underground sensor networks: research challenges. Ad Hoc Netw. J. **4**, 669–686 (2006)
3. Akyildiz, I.F., Sun, Z., Vuran, M.C.: Signal propagation techniques for wireless underground communication networks. Phys. Commun. J. (Elsevier) **2**(3), 167–183 (2009)
4. Bjornson, E., Bengtsson, M., Ottersten, B.: Optimal multiuser transmit beamforming: a difficult problem with a simple solution structure. IEEE Sig. Process. Mag. **31**(4), 142–148 (2014)
5. Bogena, H.R., Herbst, M., Huisman, J.A., Rosenbaum, U., Weuthen, A., Vereecken, H.: Potential of wireless sensor networks for measuring soil water content variability. Vadose Zone J. **9**, 1002–1013 (2010)
6. Chae, C.B., Hwang, I., Heath, R.W., Tarokh, V.: Interference aware-coordinated beamforming in a multi-cell system. IEEE Trans. Wirel. Commun. **11**(10), 3692–3703 (2012)
7. Dong, X., Vuran, M.C.: A channel model for wireless underground sensor networks using lateral waves. In: Proceedings of IEEE Globecom 2011, Houston, TX, December 2011
8. Dong, X., Vuran, M.C., Irmak, S.: Autonomous precision agriculture through integration of wireless underground sensor networks with center pivot irrigation systems. Ad Hoc Netw. **11**(7), 1975–1987 (2013)
9. Fenn, A., Hurst, P.: Ultrawideband Phased Array Antenna Technology for Sensing and Communications Systems. MIT Press, Cambridge (2015)
10. Guo, H., Sun, Z.: Channel and energy modeling for self-contained wireless sensor networks in oil reservoirs. IEEE Trans. Wirel. Commun. **13**(4), 2258–2269 (2014)
11. Konda, A., et al.: Soft microreactors for the deposition of conductive metallic traces on planar, embossed, and curved surfaces. Adv. Funct. Mater. **28**(40), 1803020 (2018)
12. Markham, A., Trigoni, N.: Magneto-inductive networked rescue system (miners): taking sensor networks underground. In: Proceedings of the 11th ICPS, IPSN 2012, pp. 317–328. ACM (2012)
13. Proakis, J., Salehi, M.: Digital Communications, 5th edn. McGraw-Hill, New York (2007)
14. Salam, A., Vuran, M.C.: Impacts of soil type and moisture on the capacity of multicarrier modulation in internet of underground things. In: Proceedings of ICCCN 2016, Waikoloa, Hawaii, USA, August 2016
15. Salam, A.: Pulses in the sand: long range and high data rate communication techniques for next generation wireless underground networks. ETD collection for University of Nebraska - Lincoln (AAI10826112) (2018). http://digitalcommons.unl.edu/dissertations/AAI10826112
16. Salam, A.: A comparison of path loss variations in soil using planar and dipole antennas. In: 2019 IEEE International Symposium on Antennas and Propagation. IEEE, July 2019
17. Salam, A.: A path loss model for through the soil wireless communications in digital agriculture. In: 2019 IEEE International Symposium on Antennas and Propagation. IEEE, July 2019

18. Salam, A.: Underground environment aware MIMO design using transmit and receive beamforming in internet of underground things. In: 2019 International Conference on Internet of Things (ICIOT 2019), San Diego, USA, June 2019
19. Salam, A.: An underground radio wave propagation prediction model for digital agriculture. Information **10**(4) (2019). http://www.mdpi.com/2078-2489/10/4/147
20. Salam, A.: Underground soil sensing using subsurface radio wave propagation. In: 5th Global Workshop on Proximal Soil Sensing, Columbia, MO, May 2019
21. Salam, A., Shah, S.: Internet of things in smart agriculture: enabling technologies. In: 2019 IEEE 5th World Forum on Internet of Things (WF-IoT) (WF-IoT 2019), Limerick, Ireland, April 2019
22. Salam, A., Shah, S.: Urban underground infrastructure monitoring IoT: the path loss analysis. In: 2019 IEEE 5th World Forum on Internet of Things (WF-IoT) (WF-IoT 2019), Limerick, Ireland, April 2019
23. Salam, A., Vuran, M.C.: EM-based wireless underground sensor networks. In: Pamukcu, S., Cheng, L. (eds.) Underground Sensing, pp. 247–285. Academic Press, Boston (2018). http://www.sciencedirect.com/science/article/pii/B9780128031391000059
24. Salam, A., Vuran, M.C., Dong, X., Argyropoulos, C., Irmak, S.: A theoretical model of underground dipole antennas for communications in internet of underground things. IEEE Trans. Antennas Propag. **67**(6), 3996–4009 (2019)
25. Salam, A., Vuran, M.C., Irmak, S.: Di-sense: in situ real-time permittivity estimation and soil moisture sensing using wireless underground communications. Comput. Netw. **151**, 31–41 (2019). http://www.sciencedirect.com/science/article/pii/S1389128618303141
26. Salam, A., Vuran, M.C.: Smart underground antenna arrays: a soil moisture adaptive beamforming approach. In: Proceedings of IEEE INFOCOM 2017, Atlanta, USA, May 2017
27. Salam, A., Vuran, M.C.: Wireless underground channel diversity reception with multiple antennas for internet of underground things. In: Proceedings of IEEE ICC 2017, Paris, France, May 2017
28. Salam, A., Vuran, M.C., Irmak, S.: Pulses in the sand: impulse response analysis of wireless underground channel. In: Proceedings of IEEE INFOCOM 2016, San Francisco, USA, April 2016
29. Salam, A., Vuran, M.C., Irmak, S.: Towards internet of underground things in smart lighting: a statistical model of wireless underground channel. In: Proceedings of 14th IEEE International Conference on Networking, Sensing and Control (IEEE ICNSC), Calabria, Italy, May 2017
30. Sun, Z., Akyildiz, I.: Channel modeling and analysis for wireless networks in underground mines and road tunnels. IEEE Trans. Commun. **58**, 1758–1768 (2010)
31. Sun, Z., et al.: MISE-PIPE: MI based wireless sensor networks for underground pipeline monitoring. Ad Hoc Netw. **9**, 218–227 (2011)
32. Sun, Z., Wang, P., Vuran, M.C., Al-Rodhaan, M.A., Al-Dhelaan, A.M., Akyildiz, I.F.: Border patrol through advanced wireless sensor networks. Ad Hoc Netw. **9**(3), 468–477 (2011)
33. Temel, S., Vuran, M.C., Lunar, M.M., Zhao, Z., Salam, A., Faller, R.K., Stolle, C.: Vehicle-to-barrier communication during real-world vehicle crash tests. Comput. Commun. **127**, 172–186 (2018). http://www.sciencedirect.com/science/article/pii/S0140366417305224
34. Tiusanen, M.J.: Soil scouts: description and performance of single hop wireless underground sensor nodes. Ad Hoc Netw. **11**(5), 1610–1618 (2013)

35. Vuran, M.C., Salam, A., Wong, R., Irmak, S.: Internet of underground things in precision agriculture: architecture and technology aspects. Ad Hoc Netw. **81**, 160–173 (2018). http://www.sciencedirect.com/science/article/pii/S1570870518305067
36. Vuran, M.C., Salam, A., Wong, R., Irmak, S.: Internet of underground things: sensing and communications on the field for precision agriculture. In: 2018 IEEE 4th World Forum on Internet of Things (WF-IoT) (WF-IoT 2018), Singapore, February 2018

Evaluation of Heterogeneous Scheduling Algorithms for Wavefront and Tile Parallelism in Video Coding

Natalia Panagou[1], Maria Koziri[1], Panos K. Papadopoulos[2],
Panagiotis Oikonomou[1], Nikos Tziritas[1], Kostas Kolomvatsos[3],
Thanasis Loukopoulos[2(✉)], and Samee U. Khan[4]

[1] Computer Science and Telecommunications Department,
University of Thessaly, Volos, Greece
{napanagou,mkoziri,paikonom,nitziri}@uth.gr
[2] Computer Science and Biomedical Informatics Department,
University of Thessaly, Volos, Greece
{ppapadopoulos,luke}@uth.gr
[3] Informatics and Telecommunications Department,
University of Athens, Athens, Greece
kostasks@di.uoa.gr
[4] Electrical and Computer Engineering Department,
North Dakota State University, Fargo, ND, USA
samee.khan@ndsu.edu

Abstract. Video is by far the "biggest" Big Data, stretching network and storage capacity to their limits. To handle the situation, video compression has been an active field of study for many years, producing output of huge commercial interest, e.g., MPEG-2 and DVD. However, video coding is a computationally expensive process and for this reason, parallelization was proposed at various granularity levels. Of particular interest, are block level methods implemented in HEVC (High Efficiency Video Coding) which was designed to be the successor of H.264/AVC for the 4K era. Parallelization in HEVC is supported by the following three modes: slices, tiles and wavefront. While considerable research was conducted on the parallelization options of HEVC, it was focused on the case of homogeneous processors. In this paper we consider video coding parallelization when the processing elements are heterogeneous. In particular, we focus on wavefront and tile parallelism and measure the performance of scheduling schemes for the induced subtasks. Through simulation experiments with dataset values obtained from common benchmark sequences, we conclude on the relevant merits of the evaluated scheduling algorithms.

Keywords: Scheduling · Heterogeneous processors · Video coding ·
Parallelism · Wavefront · Tiles · HEVC

1 Introduction

As we are rapidly moving towards realizing fully interconnected smart IoT environments at a large scale, many challenges are being posed. Of particular importance is data collection and stream processing [1] which consumes both network and

© Springer Nature Switzerland AG 2019
V. Issarny et al. (Eds.): ICIOT 2019, LNCS 11519, pp. 16–27, 2019.
https://doi.org/10.1007/978-3-030-23357-0_2

computational resources. Among all data sources, video feeds from street cameras and mobile smart devices, undoubtedly pose the "biggest" Big data size wise. As an example, Cisco indicated in [2] that video related traffic accounted for 55% of the total mobile traffic in 2015 and was increased by 75% compared to the previous year. Such trends will likely remain in the foreseeable future due to the wide use of 4K in smart phone cameras and TV sets. Therefore, in order to efficiently deploy intelligent video processing applications, e.g., car plate recognition [3] etc., as components of a smart IoT ecosystem, it is of paramount importance to reduce the size of video streams without affecting quality (referred to as video compression or video coding).

One of the most successful video coding standards is the popular H.264/AVC [4] which was designed to tackle the challenges of the FullHD era. Nevertheless, with the dawn of 4K resolutions H.264/AVC saw its age, resulting in the development of a new generation of video coding standards. Examples consist of High Efficiency Video Coding-HEVC [5] (also termed H.265) by the MPEG group in 2012, VP9 [6] by Google in 2013 and the recently launched AV1 [7] by AOMedia. Simultaneously, the successor of HEVC, termed VVC (Versatile Video Coding) or H.266 [8] is under development and scheduled for release in 2020. While the battle for the succession of H.264/AVC still wages, what is common on the newer standards is the fact that they offer improved compression ratio (for the same quality) compared to H.264/AVC. Nevertheless, to achieve such performance improvement, particularly for 4K compression, increased computational cost is involved which can only be alleviated through parallelism.

In the relevant literature parallelism was applied at various granularity levels of the video coding process such as: (i) within a block of pels (e.g., at the motion estimation or filtering steps [9]); (ii) at a block or group of blocks level (e.g., slice parallelism [10]) and (iii) at a frame level (e.g., by assigning different Groups of Pictures (GOPs) to different processors [11]). With the exception of the coarser granularity level (per GOP) most of the relevant literature on video coding parallelism assumed a homogeneous set of processors. Nevertheless, heterogeneous computing scenarios are becoming more and more important, e.g., with big.LITTLE processors [12]. In this paper we turn our attention to block level video coding parallelism assuming heterogeneous processors. Since a number of works, e.g., [13], outlined that among the parallelization granules implemented in HEVC (slices, tiles and wavefront), the last two offer the best coding performance we restrict our study to tile and wavefront parallelism.

In normal mode, the encoding of the blocks of a frame (termed Coding Tree Units-CTUs in HEVC) is done in raster order (row by row). In wavefront, CTU encodings are again done from left to right but different CTU rows can be processed in parallel, as long as the following constraint is respected: a CTU can commence encoding once the upper and upper-right CTUs are encoded. Figure 1 provides an example whereby the greyed CTUs are the ones that are already encoded. Clearly, by considering each CTU coding as a separate task, the encoding of a frame can be modeled as a DAG (Directed Acyclic Graph). Thus, in order to complete the frame's encoding at the minimum possible time, suitable scheduling algorithms are important, particularly in the presence of heterogeneity.

Similarly, efficient scheduling can prove useful in the case of tile parallelism where a frame is split into a grid of rectangular areas (tiles) comprised of multiple CTUs (see

Fig. 1. Example of wavefront parallelism with 8 threads (Kimono sequence).

Fig. 2. Example of partitioning a frame into 12 tiles (Kimono sequence).

Fig. 2). Since the encoding of each tile is independent from others, independent task (tile) scheduling techniques are applicable. Even if a plethora of results exist on task scheduling (e.g., see [14] for a comparative study), the particular case of scheduling algorithms for video coding parallelism was typically overlooked.

Our primary contribution rests on evaluating scheduling algorithms for wavefront and tile parallelism under heterogeneous assumptions concerning processors' computational power. The evaluation is based on simulation experiments using a realistic dataset for CTU coding times, obtained by encoding common test video sequences [15] using the HM 16.15 reference encoder [16] of HEVC. Results indicate that compared to random scheduling decisions (as is the current practice by many encoders) reduction in makespan of even 50% is achievable. To the best of our knowledge this is the first paper tackling heterogeneous scheduling in video coding at a finer granule than the GOP level.

The rest of the paper is organized as follows. Section 2 discusses related work. Problem details together with the DAG formulation and the tested scheduling schemes are presented in Sect. 3. Performance evaluation results are illustrated in Sect. 4 together with a summary of our findings. Finally, Sect. 5 includes our concluding remarks.

2 Related Work

HEVC offers three main parallelization approaches within a frame: wavefront, slices and tiles. Significant research exists for all three approaches. A comparative study examining the strengths of each one is provided in [13]. As it is demonstrated, in terms of quality and bitrate, wavefront is the winner. However, the achievable speedup from parallelization is rather restricted due to task precedence constraints. Furthermore, both slices and tiles provide other complementary strengths. Slices are essentially encoded as sub-frames, therefore they provide flexibility in the network transmission layer at the expense of higher header overhead, thus increased bitrate. Tiles on the other hand, allow for fine tuning the encoding parameters, e.g., the selected QP (quantization parameter), so as to increase video quality at ROIs (Regions of Interest).

In terms of slice and tile level parallelism most existing works assume homogeneous processors. In [17] the achievable speedup from slice parallelism was evaluated for HEVC assuming uniform static slice partitions. Adaptive slice resizing was discussed in [10] and [18]. The core idea was to estimate the time complexity for encoding each Macroblock/CTU of the next frame and based on these estimations resize slices to evenly distribute workload. In [10] CTU time estimation was done using weighted past average of the actual encoding times experienced in previous frames, while [18] provided a more sophisticated estimator tuned for Low Delay (LD) encodings that take advantage of GOP hierarchy.

A similar estimator to the one of [18] was used in [19] with the aim of feeding a tile resizing algorithm. The algorithm itself was based on iteratively applying the optimal one dimensional array partitioning algorithm [20] across the two frame dimensions. In [21] the authors considered tile and slice resizing based on a CTU cost estimation that used a weighting function that takes into account CTU encoding mode and depth. The tile resizing scheme was based on first defining a master tile size, apply it in one of the four frame corners and build the remaining grid using this first tile definition as basis.

The aforementioned research assumed a one on one slice/tile to homogeneous processor assignment in which case evenly splitting expected slice/tile workload is the crucial factor, while scheduling decisions are trivial. In [22] the authors proposed to increase the number of tiles a frame is split into so as to exceed the number of available processors. In this way the task granule is effectively reduced allowing for better load balancing. Tile partitioning was done in a static manner and processor assignment was performed by a greedy bin packing heuristic. Although the achievable speedup was increased compared to the one on one tile-processor assignment, using too many tiles results in lowering video quality as indicated in [23] where the authors provide experimental results on the "optimal" number of tiles that should be used given the number of available processors. Finally, in [24] the authors propose a fast heuristic to

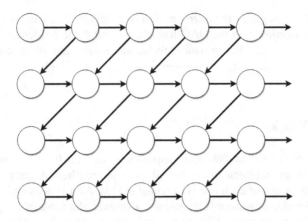

Fig. 3. Example of a wavefront DAG.

adapt tile size in case more tiles exist than processors. The heuristic is based on iteratively reducing the load of the most loaded processor by shrinking the area of one of its assigned tiles.

Overall, the case where fewer processors than tiles exist, gives rise to scheduling issues. Nevertheless, all the aforementioned works studied the case of homogeneous processors, whereas the focus of this paper is on heterogeneous processors both for tile and for wavefront parallelism.

3 Scheduling Heuristics

3.1 Formulation

Since video coding tasks are CPU bound we decided to adopt a simple model for heterogeneity that is based solely on processor speed. Let T_i denote the running time of the ith encoding task (assuming a total order of them) over a baseline processor. Let processor speedup (SP_j) denote how faster the jth processor is in running video coding tasks compared to the baseline processor. Calculating the running time of the ith task on the jth processor is done as follows:

$$Time_{ij} = T_i/SP_j \qquad (1)$$

In the experiments we assume a one on one task processor mapping. In case multiple tasks should be allocated for execution on a particular processing core, we assume a FCFS policy and calculate task completion times accordingly.

Under tile level parallelism each tile is considered a separate encoding task. Notice, that these tasks are independent. In wavefront parallelism, each task corresponds to the encoding of a single CTU. In order for a CTU compression to commence, the upper and upper right CTUs as well as the left CTU (that resides in the same row) must have finished compression. These dependencies can be captured by means of a DAG. Figure 3 illustrates the DAG structure for an example 4×5 CTU grid.

3.2 Heuristics

We evaluated two scheduling heuristics for tile parallelism namely, MaxMin and MinMin. Given a set of available tasks, i.e., tasks that can commence immediately, MaxMin selects the heaviest task and assigns it to the processor where it will experience the earliest completion time. MinMin also performs a similar processor assignment, i.e., based on earliest completion time, but starts by assigning the most lightweight task first. Notice, that in tile parallelism all tasks are available for execution at the beginning of the process.

MaxMin and MinMin heuristics were also evaluated for wavefront parallelism, with tasks becoming available depending on DAG constraints. Furthermore, we also evaluated two other heuristics that are inspired by the DAG structure namely, MaxMin-Row and MinMin-Row. These heuristics work in a similar manner to MaxMin and MinMin with the exception being that instead of ordering tasks depending on estimated load, they order tasks according to the CTU row they reside. MaxMin-Row selects tasks in a lowest row first fashion and MinMin-Row does the opposite.

Table 1. Video sequences.

Name	Resolution	Total frames	CTUs per frame
PeopleOnStreet	2560 × 1600	150	1000
Traffic	2560 × 1600	150	1000
BasketballDrive	1920 × 1080	500	510
BQTerrace	1920 × 1080	600	510
Cactus	1920 × 1080	500	510
Kimono	1920 × 1080	240	510
ParkScene	1920 × 1080	240	510

4 Experiments

4.1 Simulation Setup

We used class A and class B common test sequences [15] with characteristics described in Table 1. We encoded the sequences using the HM 16.15 reference software [16]. Low Delay setting was selected with an initial I frame followed by P frames. The remaining parameters were as follows: GOP size = 4, CTU size = 64 × 64, bit depth = 4, max CTU partitioning depth = 4, QP = 32 and search method was TZ search. These parameters are commonly used in the related literature, e.g., [17, 18] and [19]. Video compression tasks were performed on a Linux machine with Intel Xeon E5-2650 processor running at 2.2 GHz.

We recorded the time it took to compress each CTU in all the frames of a particular sequence. We should mention that the aggregation of these times differed from the total encoding time spent by at most 5%. In the experiments, the values obtained from the actual coding of the video sequences constituted the performance of the baseline processor. In practice, CTU compression times can be estimated before the encoding of

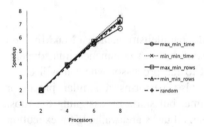

Fig. 4. Wavefront speedup (PeopleOnStreet sequence).

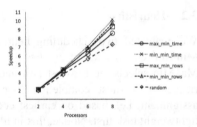

Fig. 5. Wavefront speedup (Traffic sequence).

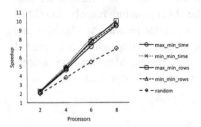

Fig. 6. Wavefront speedup (BasketballDrive sequence).

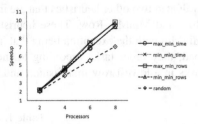

Fig. 7. Wavefront speedup (BQTerrace sequence).

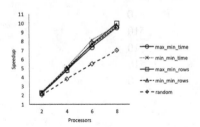

Fig. 8. Wavefront speedup (Cactus sequence).

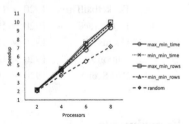

Fig. 9. Wavefront speedup (Kimono sequence).

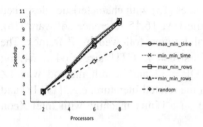

Fig. 10. Wavefront speedup (ParkScene sequence).

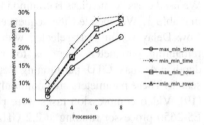

Fig. 11. Improvement over random (average of all sequences).

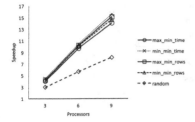

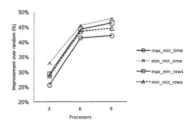

Fig. 12. Wavefront speedup (average for all sequences, processor speedups: 1, 2, 4).

Fig. 13. Improvement over random (average for all sequences, processor speedups: 1, 2, 4).

a frame commences by one of the estimators proposed in the literature. In the paper the estimator used in [19] for LowDelay coding is adopted. Under the scheme, statistics from the first GOP (4 frames) are obtained, before being able to estimate the rest. For this reason, we only record the performance of scheduling schemes from the 5th frame onwards.

4.2   Wavefront Experiments

In a first experiment we evaluated the performance of the scheduling heuristics together with random scheduling, whereby each available task is assigned to one of the processors with probability following a uniform distribution. Figures 4, 5, 6, 7, 8, 9 and 10 plot the speedup from wavefront parallelization achieved for different number of processors assuming that half of them had processor speedup = 1 (baseline processor) and the other half processor speedup = 2 (i.e., twice fast to the baseline). As it can be observed, with the notable exception of PeopleOnStreet sequence, random scheduling has clearly worst performance compared to the other 4 options. It should be noted that in PeopleOnStreet sequence there exists avid movement throughout the frame thus, most CTU codings are equally complex and for this reason random choices perform in par with the remaining heuristics. It should also be noted that the achievable speedup in many cases exceeds the available processors. This is due to the way speedup is calculated: *Speedup = SequentialTime/ParallelTime*, whereby sequential time corresponds to the performance with processor speedup = 1 (in the experiments half of the processors are twice fast).

In order to better illustrate the overall performance of the heuristics we plot the improvement over random calculated as: *(TimeRandom-TimeHeuristic)/TimeRandom*. Figure 11 shows the average performance improvement (time reduction percentage) exhibited in all sequences. As it can be observed the MinMin heuristic is a clear winner followed by the heuristic that selects CTUs giving priority to the lowest CTU row.

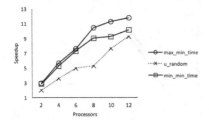

Fig. 14. Tile speedup (3 × 4 tiles, average for all sequences, processor speedups: 1, 2, static tile sizing).

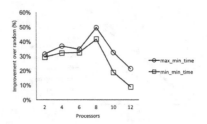

Fig. 15. Improvement over u_random (3 × 4 tiles, average for all sequences, processor speedups: 1, 2, static tile sizing).

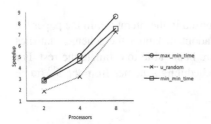

Fig. 16. Tile speedup (3 × 3 tiles, average for all sequences, processor speedups: 1, 2, static tile sizing).

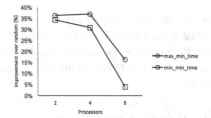

Fig. 17. Improvement over u_random (3 × 3 tiles, average for all sequences, processor speedups: 1, 2, static tile sizing).

To further confirm our findings, we run an experiment whereby 1/3rd of the processors had speedup of 1, 1/3rd speedup of 2 and another 1/3rd a speedup of 4. This scenario accounts for more heterogeneity. Thus, it is not surprising that the performance gap between random scheduling and the rest widens as shown in Fig. 12 which shows the achievable parallelization speedups and Fig. 13 which shows the performance improvement over random. Again notice that MinMin achieves the best performance reaching more than 45% of improvement, i.e., encodings are finished in almost half the time compared to random.

4.3   Tile Experiments

Next we evaluated the performance of MaxMin and MinMin on tile parallelism. We conducted experiments with tile partitioning of 3 × 4 and 3 × 3. Figures 14, 15, 16 and 17 plot the relevant performance results for the two cases. For comparison reasons we considered a modified random scheduling (u_Random) which assigns the same number of tiles on each processor but does so in a random uniform manner.

Results show that MaxMin and MinMin outperform for the largest part u_Random. Contrary to wavefront parallelism, MaxMin is the winner in tile parallelism. The performance difference between MaxMin, MinMin and u_Random is shown to initially rise as the number of processors increases, exhibits a peak and then drops as the number of processors tends to equal the number of tiles. Among MaxMin and MinMin,

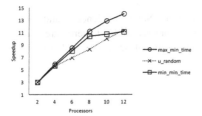

Fig. 18. Tile speedup (3 × 4 tiles, average for all sequences, processor speedups: 1, 2, adaptive tile sizing).

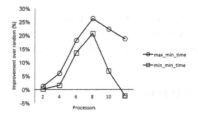

Fig. 19. Improvement over u_random (3 × 4 tiles, average for all sequences, processor speedups: 1, 2, adaptive tile sizing).

MinMin exhibits the sharpest drop. This can be explained by considering that in the extreme case where the number of processors equal the number of tiles, it will assign to the fastest processors the least heavy task, possibly leaving the heaviest ones to be assigned to low capacity processors.

In a final experiment we wanted to test the performance of tile scheduling schemes when adaptive tile resizing is performed. For this reason, we considered a scheme that aims at balancing tile sizes in a manner similar to the one proposed in [19]. Figures 18 and 19 plot the results for 3 × 4 tile partitioning. Again MaxMin is the winner, followed by MinMin in all but the case where the number of tiles and processors are equal (notice the negative improvement over u-Random for 12 processors in Fig. 19).

5 Conclusions

In this paper we evaluated scheduling heuristics for the case of video coding using wavefront and tile level parallelism, under heterogeneous assumptions concerning the available processor computational power. This issue, although crucial to performance was typically overlooked. Results demonstrate a different winner depending on the parallelization mode, with MinMin offering the best results for the wavefront case and MaxMin be the winner for tile parallelism. Concerning wavefront parallelism, placing preference depending on the row a CTU resides, bears no additional benefits to the basic MinMin scheme. At the same time, random scheduling decisions led to significantly inferior performance overall, even doubling in certain scenarios task completion time compared to other alternatives.

Acknowledgments. Panos K. Papadopoulos was supported by scholarship from IKY (State Scholarships Foundation) funded by the Act "Strengthening Human Resources Research Potential via Doctorate Research" of the Operational Program "Human Resources Development Program, Education and Lifelong Learning", 2014-2020 co-financed by the European Social Fund (ESF) and the Greek Government.

Nikos Tziritas' Post-doctoral research was carried out with an IKY scholarship funded by the Action "Supporting Post-doctoral Researchers" from EP resources "Development of Human Resources, Education and Lifelong Learning" with priority axes 6, 8, 9 and co-funded by the European Social Fund - ESF and the Greek government.

Samee U. Khan's work was supported by (while serving at) the National Science Foundation. Any opinion, findings, and conclusions or recommendations expressed in this material are those of the authors and do not necessarily reflect the views of the National Science Foundation.

References

1. Assuncao, M.D., Silva Veith, A., Buyya, R.: Distributed data stream processing and edge computing: a survey on resource elasticity and future directions. J. Netw. Comput. Appl. **103**, 1–17 (2018)
2. Cisco Systems Inc.: Cisco Visual Networking Index: Global Mobile Data Traffic Forecast Update, 2015–2020 (White Paper). http://www.cisco.com/c/en/us/solutions/collateral/service-provider/visual-networking-index-vni/mobile-white-paper-c11-520862.html
3. Anagnostopoulos, C.N., Anagnostopoulos, I., Psoroulas, I.D., Loumos, V., Kayafas, E.: License plate recognition from still images and video sequences: a survey. IEEE Trans. Intell. Transp. Syst. **9**(3), 377–391 (2008)
4. Wiegand, T., Sullivan, G.J., Bjontegaard, G., Luthra, A.: Overview of the H. 264/AVC video coding standard. IEEE Trans. Circuits Syst. Video Technol. **13**(7), 560–576 (2003)
5. Sullivan, G.J., Ohm, J.R., Han, W.J., Wiegand, T., et al.: Overview of the high efficiency video coding (HEVC) standard. IEEE Trans. Circuits Syst. Video Technol. **22**(12), 1649–1668 (2012)
6. De Cock, J., Mavlankar, A., Moorthy, A., Aaron, A.: A large-scale video codec comparison of x264, x265 and libvpx for practical VOD applications, p. 997116, September 2016
7. Alliance for Open Media. http://aomedia.org
8. Versatile Video Coding (VVC). https://jvet.hhi.fraunhofer.de
9. Hojati, E., Franche, J., Coulombe, S., Vzquez, C.: Massively parallel rateconstrained motion estimation using multiple temporal predictors in HEVC. In: 2017 IEEE International Conference on Multimedia and Expo (ICME), pp. 43–48 (2017)
10. Zhao, L., Xu, J., Zhou, Y., Ai, M.: A dynamic slice control scheme for slice-parallel video encoding. In: 2012 19th IEEE International Conference on Image Processing, pp. 713–716 (2012)
11. Rodriguez, A., Gonzalez, A., Malumbres, M.P.: Hierarchical parallelization of an H. 264/AVC video encoder. In: International Symposium on Parallel Computing in Electrical Engineering (PARELEC 2006), pp. 363–368 (2006)
12. Geng, Y., Yang, Y., Cao, G.: Energy-efficient computation offloading for multicore-based mobile devices. In: 2018 IEEE Conference on Computer Communications (INFOCOM), pp. 46–54 (2018)
13. Chi, C.C., et al.: Parallel scalability and efficiency of HEVC parallelization approaches. IEEE Trans. Circuits Syst. Video Technol. **22**(12), 1827–1838 (2012)
14. Chandio, A.A., et al.: A comparative study on resource allocation and energy efficient job scheduling strategies in large-scale parallel computing systems. Cluster Comput. **17**, 1349–1367 (2014)
15. Bossen, F.: Common test conditions and software reference configurations. Document JCTVC-H1100, JCT-VC, San Jose, CA, February 2012
16. HM 16.15 Reference Software. http://hevc.hhi.fraunhofer.de
17. Pinol, P., Gomis, H.M., Lopez, O., Malumbres, M.P.: Slice-based parallel approach for HEVC encoder. J. Supercomput. **71**, 1882–1892 (2014)

18. Koziri, M., Papadopoulos, P., Tziritas, N., Dadaliaris, A.N., Loukopoulos, T., Khan, S.U.: Slice-based parallelization in HEVC encoding: realizing the potential through efficient load balancing. In: 2016 IEEE 18th International Workshop on Multimedia Signal Processing (MMSP), pp. 1–6 (2016)
19. Koziri, M., et al.: Heuristics for tile parallelism in HEVC. In: 2017 25th European Signal Processing Conference (EUSIPCO), pp. 1514–1518 (2017)
20. Mingozzi, A., Ricciardelli, S., Spadoni, M.: Partitioning a matrix to minimize the maximum cost. Discrete Appl. Math. **62**(1–3), 221–248 (1995)
21. Ahn, Y.J., Hwang, T.J., Sim, D.G., Han, W.J.: Implementation of fast HEVC encoder based on SIMD and data-level parallelism. EURASIP J. Image Video Process. **2014**(1), 16 (2014)
22. Shafique, M., Khan, M.U.K., Henkel, J.: Power efficient and workload balanced tiling for parallelized high efficiency video coding. In: 2014 IEEE International Conference on Image Processing (ICIP), pp. 1253–1257. IEEE (2014)
23. Malossi, G., Palomino, D., Diniz, C., Susin, A., Bampi, S.: Adjusting video tiling to available resources in a per-frame basis in high efficiency video coding. In: 2016 14th IEEE International New Circuits and Systems Conference (NEWCAS), pp. 1–4. IEEE (2016)
24. Papadopoulos, P.K., Koziri, M., Loukopoulos, T.: A fast heuristic for tile partitioning and processor assignment in HEVC. In: 2018 25th IEEE International Conference on Image Processing (ICIP), pp. 4143–4147 (2018)

A Method to Secure IoT Devices Against Botnet Attacks

Trusit Shah[✉] and Subbarayan Venkatesan[✉]

The University of Texas at Dallas, Richardson, TX 75080, USA
{trusit.shah,venky}@utdallas.edu

Abstract. An unsecured or weak authentication system between an IoT device and a user provides opportunities to attackers to manipulate and use the IoT device as botnet. The proliferation of IoT devices with an unsecured/weak authentication mechanism has increased the threat of using a huge number of IoT devices as botnets for large-scale DDoS attacks. Default credential pairs (like 'root-root' or 'admin-admin') for the Telnet or SSH connections are still part of a large group of IoT products, and many malwares have exploited this vulnerability to capture a large number of IoT devices and use them as botnets. In the recent past, Mirai malware had infected roughly a million IoT devices at its peak by brute-forcing just 62 pairs of default credentials. In this paper, we present a concept called 'login puzzle' to prevent capture of IoT devices in a large scale. Login puzzle is a variant of client puzzle, which presents a puzzle to the remote device during the login process to prevent unrestricted log-in attempts. Login puzzle is a set of multiple mini puzzles with a variable complexity, which the remote device is required to solve before logging into any IoT device. Every unsuccessful log-in attempt increases the complexity of solving the login puzzle for the next attempt. In this paper, we have introduced a novel mechanism to change the complexity of puzzle after every unsuccessful login attempt. If each IoT device had used login puzzle, Mirai attack would have required almost two months to acquire devices, while it acquired them in 20 h.

Keywords: IoT security · DDoS attacks · Client puzzles · Botnet

1 Introduction

In the last decade, the rapid growth of IoT products in the market have connected billions of small-scale devices to the internet. To survive in such a fast-growing market, developers often neglects security aspects and release vulnerable products in the market. The attackers use such vulnerabilities to perform large-scale DDoS attacks and steal personal information of the user. Mirai is a well-known DDoS attack, which represents the first type of attack using vulnerable IoT devices [21]. A casino at Las Vegas, which lost some of its critical information due to a cyber-attack enabled by a vulnerable internet enabled fish tank[1], is an example of another attack.

---

[1] https://www.businessinsider.com/hackers-stole-a-casinos-database-through-a-thermometer-in-the-lobby-fish-tank-2018-4.

© Springer Nature Switzerland AG 2019
V. Issarny et al. (Eds.): ICIOT 2019, LNCS 11519, pp. 28–42, 2019.
https://doi.org/10.1007/978-3-030-23357-0_3

IoT devices with either default or easy to guess credentials allow the attackers to access these devices remotely with root permissions. Attacker use a pre-defined set of credentials to log in open Telnet or SSH ports. Most of the time, around 100 credentials are sufficient to capture a massive number of IoT devices and only a few seconds are needed to brute-force these credentials. Thus, a self-replicating attacker script can brute-force a few hundred thousand devices in less than a week. The ability to brute force devices without any restriction enables attackers to capture a large number of IoT botnets.

A potential solution for this problem is to restrict a single IP from trying a large number of login attempts. This solution is vulnerable to IP address hopping [22]: an attacker can change the IP address after every unsuccessful login. Another solution is to implement a blocking mechanism, which allows a small number of login attempts before it blocks further login attempts. This method certainly reduces the number of devices being captured, but the attacker script can get an instantaneous access till it reaches the blocking number. A selective approach with different login credentials for different kind of devices can capture a large number of devices. A timeout-based method is also useful in preventing multiple abusive login attempts. The device enters into a timeout mode after every unsuccessful attempt and every unsuccessful attempt increases the timeout period. The downside of the timeout method is, the attacker script can capture other devices in parallel.

In this paper, we present a method called 'login puzzle' to prevent the unrestricted login attempts performed by a malicious script. Login puzzle is a collection of mini puzzles, which requires a fixed amount of time and computation power to solve. When a malicious script tries to brute-force an IoT device, it needs to allocate a fixed amount of time and resource to solve the login puzzle, and every unsuccessful attempt increases the complexity of the login puzzle, hence increasing the time and computation power required to solve the next login puzzle. At a certain point, the login puzzle is hard enough that it is not practical for the script to solve. This method not only limits the number of attempts but also slows down the rate of attempts. It is a combination of both blocking and timeout method and provides better performance than these individual methods.

Another approach is to send a single puzzle to the login entity instead of multiple mini puzzles, it leads to a problem in changing the complexity of the puzzle. If we change the complexity every time a wrong attempt happens, an adversary can request multiple parallel sessions with a same complexity. On the other side, a malicious script can perform multiple attempts just to increase the complexity to block a benign user. Use of login puzzle solves these problems.

Login entity must solve all the mini puzzles of the login puzzle to get the login access to the IoT device. All of these puzzles are sent sequentially; login entity will get the next mini puzzle, once it solves the previous one. In case of parallel requests, once a request solves all the puzzle and attempts an unsuccessful login attempt, number of mini puzzles for the other parallel requests will increase, consequently increasing the complexity of the subsequent login attempts. If an adversary just requests multiple sessions without actually solving mini puzzles, the complexity of the puzzle won't increase, hence benign user won't be block by any malicious script.

We have calculated the improvement achieved by using login puzzle. We have measured this scheme with Mirai and computed the amount of additional time and resource required to capture the IoT devices. The main contribution of our work includes:

- A practical mechanism to extend the capture time of an IoT device as botnet
- Introduction to the login puzzle and provide calculations for its performance efficiency
- A novel complexity changing mechanism, which ensures constant resource allocation from the client side and provides minimum penalty to benign users

This paper is organized in the following way. We discuss about previous work in Sect. 2. Section 3 describes our security mechanism followed by Sect. 4 explaining the performance analysis and comparison with other authentication mechanisms.

1.1   DDoS Attack Overview

A denial of service is characterized as 'attempt to prevent the use of a network service to the legitimate users. In a DDoS, an attacker uses multiple devices to achieve denial of service. As more IoT devices are being manufactured with limited security considerations, new methods are being introduced to use IoT devices as bots for DDoS attacks. A study by Dragan Peraković et al. shows that the number of DDoS attacks has increased with the growth in numbers of IoT devices [20].

A DDoS attack using IoT botnets typically consists of three phases: host scanning, device acquisition and denial of service attack. In the host scanning phase, the attacker scans for the IoT devices with open Telnet or SSH ports. After discovering a vulnerable device, the attacker script tries to log into the device using a set of pre-defined credentials. If the attacker gets the access to the IoT device using one of the pre-defined credentials, the attacker executes the second phase. In the device acquisition phase, a self-replicating script is injected inside the IoT device by the attacker.

The self-replicating script scans through the network to infect more IoT device using the same host scanning mechanism and injects the same script into the newly infected device. Meanwhile, this script continuously communicates with the attacking server and waits for the commands to perform a DDoS attack. After acquiring enough IoT devices, the attacking server commands all the infected IoT devices to attack a specific service. A large volume of internet traffic is generated for the victim with the potential to disrupt the service.

Figure 1 shows an underlying architecture for the DDoS attack using IoT botnets. The four main components for a DDoS attack using IoT devices are an attacker, a malware server, a command and control (CnC) server and IoT botnets. The attacker initiates the host scanning phase and acquires an ample amount of IoT devices. Those discovered IoT devices download the self-replicating script from the malware server. In some cases, the malware server is also known as report server. The script registers the IoT device to the CnC server and waits for the command from the CnC server. Finally, after acquiring adequate bots, the attacker commands the CnC server to send a request to botnets to attack the victim service.

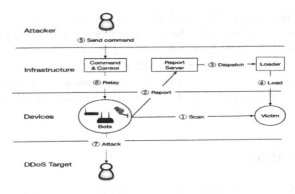

Fig. 1. Mirai architecture

2 Previous Work

Researchers have proposed few methods to use digital problems to avoid DDoS attacks. Most of these works secure server or web services from a DDoS attack. The very first work was introduced by Aura et al. as client puzzle [1]. In this paper, the authors introduced the concept of resource commitment at the client side. The client solves a puzzle given by the server with the authentication, before the server allocates any heavy resource for the client. While this method is very effective in stopping the DDoS attack at server side, it doesn't provide significant improvement at the host scanning phase because it uses problems of same complexity every time. If the complexity is too high, the benign user suffers from getting access of the IoT device and if the complexity is too low, the attacker can solve it easily and can brute force credentials to get the access of the IoT device. A varying complexity method helps benign user to access IoT device with low computation and restricts an attacker from brute forcing the credentials on the IoT devices. Michalas et al. presented a similar concept in client puzzle to prevent DoS attack in an ad-hoc network [3]. Another client puzzle was introduced by Abliz et al. which protects a server from DDoS attack based on traffic created by the clients [14]. Suriadi and et al. have presented a similar approach to prevent a DoS attack for web services [2].

Many approaches for creating client puzzle have been proposed by researchers. Chen et al. have proposed a generic way to represent a client puzzle [4]. In the paper authors have defined client puzzle as a tuple algorithm, which provides a formal setup to generate puzzle, solve puzzle and formal verification of the puzzle. Groza et al. have presented a formal verification for the puzzle hardness and bounds [5]. Jing et al. have used repeated squaring and hash reversal client-puzzle with the leaky bucket algorithm [6].

Other than client puzzle, various security strategies at different stages of DDoS attack have been proposed by researchers to prevent the DDoS attacks [12, 13]. At the discovery stage, a DDoS attack can be prevented by closing the unused ports. At the network level, construction of a firewall restricts the spread of malware. IoT devices are made for performing specific tasks and require communication with specific domains only. Continuous monitoring of running processes and network traffic of an IoT device provides enhanced security. This method constrains device activities and network traffic and causes false alarms when benign but unknown activities are happening.

Various methods have been introduced by different researchers to prevent the DDoS attack on the victim side. There are methods called intrusion detection to detect a potential DDoS attack. There are other signature-based methods to detect the intrusion [16, 19]. Recently, machine learning based detection methods have been proposed to check the spread of the DDoS attack [17, 18].

3 Our Methodology

We present a mechanism to provide security against the DDoS attack at the device scan phase. The malware could acquire a large number of IoT devices because there is no restriction on trying multiple guessed credentials using a brute force attack. Our method called 'Login puzzle', prevents an attacker from brute-forcing credentials. Login puzzle provides an extra layer of a challenge-response mechanism by generating NP-hard puzzles and asks the login entity to solve it before being logged in. The difficulty of question gets harder with the number of false attempts, hence stopping the intruder from using the brute-force method to capture an IoT device.

The login attempts to an IoT device can be divided into three main categories: log in using user interface having username-password as security credentials, log in using script having username-password as security credentials and log in using script using the digital certificate as security credentials. The third category is not vulnerable to brute force attack as it is computationally impossible to create a brute-force attack on a digital certificate, hence no additional security required for this category. For the first and second categories, an additional mechanism is required to prevent the unrestricted brute-force login attempt. In our methodology, we use regular captcha and login puzzle for the first and second category, respectively.

Both first and second category use: username-password as security credential: To differentiate them, a flag bit indicating the type is sent along with the login request. In this paper, we assume that a computer program is not capable of solving the regular captcha used for login. Hence, if a script tries to fake itself as a human to avoid the login puzzle, it won't be able to login to the system.

3.1 Login Puzzle

A login puzzle is a collection of mini puzzles with a varying complexity, which require a fixed amount of time and resource to solve depending on the complexity. A login puzzle is defined as $P(n)$, where n defines the complexity of the puzzle. Complexity of a login puzzle is addition of all of its mini puzzles. Mini puzzle is expressed as $M(x, n)$, where x is the set of puzzle parameters, n is the complexity of the mini puzzle. A login puzzle can have mini puzzles with different complexities. The time required to solve the login puzzle P and mini puzzle M at complexity n is $t_p(n)$ and $t_m(n)$ respectively.

A login puzzle P has following properties:

- Based on the complexity n, it requires a fixed amount of time and computation power to solve.
- For a puzzle function P, if $n_1 > n_2$ then $t_p(n_1) \geq t_p(n_2)$.
- For every device with a finite computational capacity C, $\exists$n at which computational capacity C requires unreasonably more time and resource to solve the login puzzle. This value of complexity is called critical complexity for the computational capacity C. The time require to solve it called critical time $t_c(n)$.

Complexity Increment of the Login Puzzle

After every unsuccessful attempt, the complexity of the login puzzle is increased. There are two ways the complexity can be increased: linear increment and exponential increment. In the linear increment, the complexity of login puzzle is increased exponentially. This can be achieved by either increasing the number of mini puzzles, without changing the complexity of mini puzzles or increasing the complexity of only one mini puzzle. In exponential increment, the complexity of each mini puzzle is incremented exponentially, consequently increasing the overall complexity exponentially. In general, after every unsuccessful attempt complexity of the puzzle is incremented exponentially and in case client stops attempting the puzzle, the complexity is increased linearly.

Login Puzzle in Login Mechanism

At each login attempt by a remote device, a login puzzle is sent to the device. The initial complexity of the login puzzle is 1, and each unsuccessful login attempt to the IoT device exponentially increases the complexity. As per the third property of the login puzzle, at some point, the login attempt requires immense resources, which cannot be handled by the remote login-device. The complexity increment mechanism is as follow:

- Normal attempt: When a remote login entity solves all the puzzles, it is considered as a normal attempt. Once the remote device provides solutions for all the puzzles, it has access to the login and if it performs an unsuccessful login attempt, the complexity of login puzzle is increased exponentially. On the other side, for successful login attempt the complexity will reset to 1. The first part of Fig. 2 provides illustration to this case.
- Midway give up attempt: When a login entity stops solving mini puzzles in the middle and doesn't arrive at login attempt, the login puzzle complexity is increased linearly. This can be performed by either increasing number of mini puzzles or increasing complexity of single mini puzzle. The second part of Fig. 2 represents this case.
- Parallel login attempts: This situation arises when a login entity requests for the login access during an existing login entity solving login puzzle. At the initial stage the new login entity will have same complexity as the previous one. In case the previous one does the unsuccessful login attempt, the complexity of login puzzle is doubled. Figure 3 shows the message exchange representation of this case.

The proposed method increases the complexity of the login puzzle irrespective of the IP address of the requestor. If an attacker script changes its IP address at each login attempt, it still needs to solve login puzzle with a higher complexity after every unsuccessful attempt. Thus, login puzzle is not vulnerable to IP hopping attack.

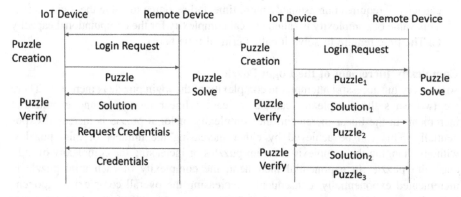

Fig. 2. The first image represents the normal login request, where the puzzle is provided to the remote device and after providing the solution remote device is able to login. The second image represents the case when remote device stops solving the puzzle after certain login attempts.

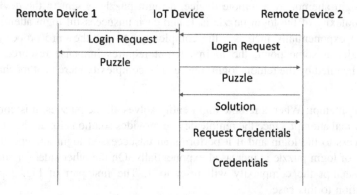

Fig. 3. This figure shows the parallel request case, in this particular case, if the remote device 2 provides wrong credentials, the complexity of remote device 1 will increase exponentially.

3.2   Resource and Timing Analysis

The resources and time required to solve a login puzzle is addition of time and resource required to solve all mini puzzles, hence we consider complexity of login puzzle for the resource and timing analysis. Every device needs to allocate a fixed computational capacity to solve a login puzzle. The required computational capacity varies based on the type and complexity of the login puzzle and, as per the 3rd property of the login puzzle, after m tries, the login puzzle reaches a certain complexity that it is not feasible for the device to solve it. Thus, a device with computational capacity C is limited to only m tries. All these m tries are not instantaneous; for every try, the device needs to solve a login puzzle, which requires a fixed amount of time to solve. In this section, we will measure the effectiveness of login puzzle on a botnet capture script, which uses x number of credentials to capture an IoT device.

The time required to try one credential without login puzzle be t_d. This time includes propagation and transmission delay caused by the network and processing delay due to login procedure; it is few milliseconds in duration. If we consider a uniform distribution of the credentials, it requires on an average $x/2$ attempts for an attacker script to capture an IoT device as a botnet if the device's credential is from one of the x credentials. The device needs to perform x failed attempts if the device's credential is not from the list. Assuming that the ratio of number of devices whose credentials are from x credentials to the total number of devices scanned is p, the average time required to capture one device is:

$$t_d * \frac{x}{2} * p + t_d * x * (1 - p)$$

This can be further simplified as:

$$x * t_d \left(1 - \frac{p}{2}\right) \tag{1}$$

Here,

$$p = \frac{number\ of\ devices\ whose\ credentials\ are\ from\ x\ credentials}{total\ number\ of\ devices\ scanned}$$

If we consider an exponentially increasing login puzzle, where the complexity of $t_p(n)$ increases 'a' times with the increment of complexity of login puzzle by 1. Considering, the time required to solve the login puzzle at complexity 1 is t_c. As per the 3rd property of login puzzle, after m attempts the problem becomes incomputable for the device. The total time required to solve login puzzle for first m attempts is,

$$t_m = \sum_{i=0}^{m-1} t_c * a^i$$

If the device's credential is from one of the pre-defined credentials, it takes $x/2$ attempts to capture the device, otherwise the attacker script tries x credentials. Considering the ratio of number of devices whose credentials are from x credentials to the total number of devices scanned is p and there are k mini puzzles in one login puzzle, average time required by a device to capture one device after using login puzzle is,

$$p * \left(t_{x/2} + \frac{x * k * t_d}{2}\right) + (1 - p) * (t_x + x * k * t_d)$$

Where,

$$t_{x/2} = \sum_{i=0}^{x/2-1} t_c * a^i \text{ and } t_x = \sum_{i=0}^{x-1} t_c * a^i$$

For the value of $x/2 < m \le x$, the t_x term in above equation becomes t_m, because after m attempts the login puzzle is incomputable.

$$p * (t_{\frac{x}{2}} + \frac{x * t_d}{2}) + (1 - p) * (t_m + x * t_d)$$

For simplicity, if we consider the time complexity of login puzzle increases with a factor of 2. The above values can be simplified as below:

$$t_m = t_c * (2^m - 1)$$

$$t_{x/2} = t_c * \left(2^{x/2} - 1\right)$$

If we assume the factor of t_c to t_d is f.
The average required time to capture a device using login puzzle is,

$$t_c * \left(2^{x/2} - 1 + \frac{x * k}{2 * f}\right) * p + t_c * \left(2^m - 1 + \frac{m * k}{f}\right) * (1 - p) \qquad (2)$$

If $m \le x/2$, $x/2$ in the first term of the above equation becomes t_m and the average time required to capture a device using login puzzle is,

$$t_c * \left(2^m - 1 + \frac{m * k}{f}\right) * p + t_c * \left(2^m - 1 + \frac{m * k}{f}\right) * (1 - p)$$

The above equation can be simplified to,

$$t_c * \left(2^m - 1 + \frac{m * k}{f}\right) \qquad (3)$$

Also, the probability of the device getting captured for all above cases is,

$$\frac{p * m}{x}$$

4   Evaluation and Performance Measure

We evaluated our approach on the different environments with different login puzzle conditions for Mirai DDoS attack. We have used three different environments with completely different capabilities to measure the effectiveness of our approach. The first environment is a small scale IoT device and we have used Raspberry Pi 3. The second environment is a MacBook Pro laptop with quad-core Intel i7 processor and 16 GB of RAM. The final environment is a cloud server hosted on AWS cloud service. The AWS instance contains 36 cores with 60 GB RAM. The first environment represents the normal spread of botnets, where infected IoT devices scan other IoT devices and solve the login puzzles themselves. The second and third environments provide the insight for the case, when IoT devices don't solve the login puzzles but send it over to the server to solve them. The primary difference between the second and third environment is the processing power of the server. The login puzzle we are using for the evaluation is as follow:

D (x, n): find a number m, for which SHA512(x ∥ m) has all last n bits are 0.

Table 1 shows the typical time required for all three environments to solve the login puzzle for complexity n.

4.1 Mirai Evaluation

Mirai was a well-known malware, which acquired more than 600k devices during its lifespan. Mirai infected 11k hosts in first 10 min of bootstrap phase and 64,500 devices in 20 h [8]. The bootstrap phase lasted for around two hours and initial 834 devices started scanning. MIRAI had comparatively a smaller number of credentials compare to other massive DDoS attacks Blaster [9] and Code Red [10]. This contributed to a slow doubling rate 75 min compare to Code Red (37 min) and Blaster (9 min) [8].

We use the following method to simplify the performance evaluation of login puzzle. First, we calculate the average time required to capture a single device with and without using login puzzle. Using these values, we measure the performance enhancement achieved by login puzzle. Finally, we multiply the performance enhancement ratio and the actual time taken by Mirai to spread over the network and compute the time required to spread Mirai when all the IoT devices are using login puzzle. We also made another assumption that the number of mini puzzles, k = 16.

Table 1. Time required to solve login puzzle for different type of devices

Environment	n	t(n)
Raspberry Pi	16	∼10 s
	24	200 s
	32	Incomputable
Macbook Pro	16	Less than a second
	24	20 s
	32	∼85 min
	40	Incomputable
AWS Server	16	Milliseconds
	24	Less than a second
	32	∼1 min
	40	∼250 min
	48	Incomputable

Number of credentials used in Mirai was 62 (x is 62 in the Eq. 1). Thus, the average time to capture one device is:

$$62 * t_d \left(1 - \frac{p}{2}\right) = 6.2 * \left(1 - \frac{p}{2}\right) \text{ in seconds} \tag{4}$$

We have tested the values of t_c and t_d for raspberry pi, and the values are 10 μs and 100 ms respectively. The factor $f = \frac{t_c}{t_d} = 10^{-4}$.

To calculate value of m, we assume that the attacker script stops solving login puzzle, once the time taken for solving captcha reaches 100 s. value of $m = \log_2\left(\frac{100\,\text{s}}{t_c}\right)$ $= 23.26 \sim 24$.

As value of the $x/2$ is greater than m, the average time required to capture one IoT device is calculated using Eq. 3,

$$t_c * \left(2^m - 1 + \frac{m * k}{f}\right) = 10^{-5} * \left(2^{24} - 1 + 24 * 16 * 10^4\right) \sim 200\,\text{s}$$

Also due to limitation of only m tries can be performed, not all devices with the default credentials can be captured.

The probability of device being captured is: $\frac{m}{x} = \frac{24}{62} = 0.39$.

Thus, with the login puzzle the number of devices captured by Mirai malware is: 64,500 * 0.39 = 24967.

Time required to capture one device using login puzzle with probability of device being captured is 1:

$$t_{(p=1)} = \frac{\textit{time required to capture one device using login puzzle}}{\textit{probability of device being captured}} = 512.82\,\text{s}$$

In conclusion, use of login puzzle increases the time required to capture a device by a factor of,

$$\frac{t_{(p=1)}}{\textit{time required to capture single device without login puzzle}} = 82.72$$

Here, the time required to capture single device without digital captcha is calculated from Eq. 4 by setting p = 0, which represents the maximum value for the equation. This implies that the total time required to cover the spread of 64,500 devices with login puzzle will be = 20 h * 82.72 $\sim$ 69 days.

Similar calculation can be performed on 2nd and 3rd type of environment and we can find time required to capture 64,500 devices if all the devices were using login puzzle and the login puzzles are solved on cloud with capabilities mentioned in Table 1. Table 2 mentions these times.

Table 2. Time required to capture 64,500 devices with login puzzle using different environment

Environment	Time required
Raspberry pi	59 days
Macbook pro	42 days
AWS Server (96 GB RAM, 64 cores)	26 days

4.2 Comparison with Blocking Method

In the blocking method, after a certain amount of attempts the IoT device blocks further login attempts until the user approves those attempts. At first, it looks like a blocking method with a small number of login attempts performs better than the login puzzle. In fact, based on our calculations, our method performs 70 times better than the blocking mechanism.

Let's assume that the IoT device blocks login attempts after b attempts. The average time required to capture one device is,

$$t_d * \frac{b}{2} * \left(\frac{b * p}{x}\right) + t_d * b * \left(1 - \frac{b * p}{x}\right)$$

The first term in the equation represents that one of the randomly guessed credentials in first b tries is the credential of the device. On an average it requires b/2 tries to achieve it with the probability b/x. This probability is finally multiplied with probability p, which represents the number of devices with the credentials used by the malware. The second term represents the scenario when the malware is not able to guess the correct credentials in first b login attempts. The above equation can be further simply to 300–7.25p milli-seconds for the value of b = 3 and x = 62. The ratio of number of devices captured to total number of devices with given credential is $\frac{b}{x} = \frac{3}{62} = 0.05$.

The value of p varies from 0 to 1 doesn't have a big impact on time required to capture the device. Thus, we can assume that the time required to capture one device is 300 ms. So, the average time to capture one device is = 300/0.05 ms = 6 s. The average time to capture one device using login puzzle is = 170/0.39 s = 436.34 s. This implies that the login puzzle method is roughly 70 times better than blocking method.

4.3 Comparison with Existing Client Puzzles

In this section, we will compare our approach with existing client puzzles and showcase its suitability to prevent the IoT device capture on a large scale. We compare our scheme with simple client puzzle and adaptive client puzzle. A simple client puzzle is the most basic form of client puzzle and adaptive puzzle is a type of puzzle which changes its complexity based on the situation. We used three parameters to compare these client puzzles: login delay, resource assurance, benign penalty.

Table 3 shows a comparison between these three client puzzles. As normal client puzzle doesn't change its complexity over the time, it is not providing any significant delay in login process. At the same time, it is not creating any high waiting time for the benign user, so benign penalty is minimum in this case. For the case of adaptive puzzle, the login delay can go really high, as the complexity go higher. As discussed in the previous sections, a malicious user can increase the complexity for the benign user by sending multiple fake requests. Just like adaptive puzzle, login puzzle has high login delay and increases with every wrong login attempt. In login puzzle, as discussed in the previous sections, puzzle ensures the resource assurance and has different policies to increase complexity for benign and malicious request, hence benign penalty is minimal in this case.

Table 3. Client puzzles comparisons

	Client puzzle	Adaptive puzzle	Login puzzle
Login delay	Very low	High	High
Resource assurance	No	No	Yes
Benign penalty	low	Very high	Minimal

5   Discussion and Future Work

Unlike normal adaptive puzzle, login puzzle doesn't have problem of benign penalty. Login puzzle provides minimal penalties to benign users. These penalties can be further reduced, if someway a benign request is differentiated from malicious request. As a future work to reduce the benign penalties, a method to provide the login puzzle only to the suspicious scripts can be implemented. There are researches explain multiple ways to differentiate a bot attack from a regular user login [7, 11, 15].

This paper assumes the distribution of the passwords is uniform, but in a real-world scenario, it is not the case. A more detailed study with a non-uniform password distribution provides a more accurate performance analysis of the login puzzle.

6   Conclusion

A large number of IoT devices with default credentials pairs or easy to guess passwords has increased the threat of Acquisition of IoT devices as botnets. In the recent past, Mirai malware has exploited this vulnerability and infected around 600 k IoT devices.

In this paper, we demonstrated how adding an extra layer of login puzzle during an authentication phase can reduce the number of IoT devices being captured as botnets. A login puzzle is an NP-hard problem, whose complexity increases at every unsuccessful login attempt. In this paper, we used 'searching a bitstream of zeros at the end of the inverse of a one-way hash function' as the login puzzle problem.

However, this method does not prevent capturing of every IoT device, it reduces the number of devices being captured and increases the time and resource required to capture those devices. Based on the calculations in Sect. 4, the additional time required to capture IoT devices is enough to detect the spread of the malware through the network traffic and prevent it from acquiring more devices.

Acknowledgements. This research was conducted at Distributed Systems Lab of The University of Texas at Dallas. We would like to thank all the anonymous reviewers for their valuable feedback to improve this paper.

References

1. Aura, T., Nikander, P., Leiwo, J.: DOS-resistant authentication with client puzzles. In: Christianson, B., Malcolm, J.A., Crispo, B., Roe, M. (eds.) Security Protocols 2000. LNCS, vol. 2133, pp. 170–177. Springer, Heidelberg (2001). https://doi.org/10.1007/3-540-44810-1_22
2. Suriadi, S., Stebila, D., Clark, A., Liu, H.: Defending web services against denial of service attacks using client puzzles. In: 2011 IEEE 9th International Conference on Web Services 2011, pp. 25–32. IEEE Computer Society (2011)
3. Michalas, A., Komninos, N., Prasad, N.R., Oleshchuk, V.A.: New client puzzle approach for dos resistance in ad hoc networks. In: 2010 IEEE International Conference on Information Theory and Information Security (ICITIS), pp. 568–573. IEEE, December 2010
4. Chen, L., Morrissey, P., Smart, N.P., Warinschi, B.: Security notions and generic constructions for client puzzles. In: Matsui, M. (ed.) ASIACRYPT 2009. LNCS, vol. 5912, pp. 505–523. Springer, Heidelberg (2009). https://doi.org/10.1007/978-3-642-10366-7_30
5. Groza, B., Warinschi, B.: Revisiting difficulty notions for client puzzles and DoS resilience. In: Gollmann, D., Freiling, F.C. (eds.) ISC 2012. LNCS, vol. 7483, pp. 39–54. Springer, Heidelberg (2012). https://doi.org/10.1007/978-3-642-33383-5_3
6. Jing, Y.K., Ming, J.T.C., Niyato, D.: Rate limiting client puzzle schemes for denial-of-service mitigation. In: 2013 IEEE Wireless Communications and Networking Conference (WCNC), pp. 1848–1853 (2013)
7. Walid, A., Mostafa, A., Salama, M.: MalNoD: malicous node discovery in internet-of-things through fingerprints. In: 2017 European Conference on Electrical Engineering and Computer Science (EECS). IEEE (2017)
8. Antonakakis, M., et al.: Understanding the Mirai botnet. In: USENIX Security Symposium (2017)
9. Bailey, M., Cooke, E., Jahanian, F., Watson, D.: The blaster worm: then and now. IEEE Secur. Priv. **3**, 26–31 (2005)
10. Moore, D., Shannon, C., Claffy, K.: Code-red: a case study on the spread and victims of an internet worm. In: 2nd ACM Internet Measurement Workshop (2002)
11. Binkley, J.R., Singh, S.: An algorithm for anomaly-based botnet detection. SRUTI **6**, 7 (2006)
12. Mirkovic, J., Dietrich, S., et al.: Internet denial of service: attack and defense mechanisms. University of Pittsburgh (2005)
13. Jiang, L., et al.: Analysis and comparison of the network security protocol with DoS/DDoS attack resistance performance. In: 2015 IEEE 17th International Conference on High Performance Computing and Communications (HPCC), 2015 IEEE 7th International Symposium on Cyberspace Safety and Security (CSS), 2015 IEEE 12th International Conference on Embedded Software and Systems (ICESS). IEEE (2015)
14. Abliz, M., Znati, T.F.: Defeating DDoS using productive puzzles. In: 2015 International Conference on Information Systems Security and Privacy (ICISSP), pp. 114–123. IEEE, February 2015

15. Gu, G., et al.: Botminer: clustering analysis of network traffic for protocol-and structure-independent botnet detection, p. 139 (2008)
16. Gu, G., Porras, P., Yegneswaran, V., Fong, M., Lee, W.: BotHunter: detecting malware infection through ids-driven dialog correlation. In: Proceedings of the 16th USENIX Security Symposium (Security 2007) (2007)
17. Saad, S., et al.: Detecting P2P botnets through network behavior analysis and machine learning. In: 2011 Ninth Annual International Conference on Privacy, Security and Trust (PST). IEEE (2011)
18. Ranjan, S., Robinson, J., Chen, F.: Machine learning based botnet detection using real-time connectivity graph based traffic features. U.S. Patent No. 8,762,298, 24 June 2014
19. Masud, M.M., Al-khateeb, T., Khan, L., Thuraisingham, B., Hamlen, K.W.: Flow-based identification of Botnet traffic by mining multiple. In: Proceedings of International Conference on Distributed Framework & Application (2008)
20. Peraković, D., et al.: Analysis of the IoT impact on volume of DDoS attacks. In: XXXIII Simpozijum o novim tehnologijama u poštanskom i telekomunikacionom saobraćaju – PosTel 2015, Beograd, 1. i 2. December 2015
21. Kolias, C., Kambourakis, G., Stavrou, A., Voas, J.: DDoS in the IoT: Mirai and other botnets. Computer **50**(7), 80–84 (2017)
22. Sifalakis, M., Schmid, S., Hutchison, D.: Network address hopping: a mechanism to enhance data protection for packet communications. In: IEEE International Conference on Communications, ICC 2005, pp. 1518–1523 (2005)

Clearer than Mud: Extending Manufacturer Usage Description (MUD) for Securing IoT Systems

Simran Singh[✉], Ashlesha Atrey, Mihail L. Sichitiu, and Yannis Viniotis

North Carolina State University, Raleigh, NC 27606, USA
{ssingh28,amatrey,mlsichit,candice}@ncsu.edu

Abstract. Internet of Things (IoT) devices, expected to increase exponentially over the next several years, are easy targets for attackers. To make these devices more secure, the IETF's draft of Manufacturer Usage Description (MUD) provides a means for the manufacturer of an IoT device to specify its intended purpose and communication patterns in terms of access control lists (ACLs), thereby defining the device's normal behaviour. However, MUD may not be sufficient to comprehensively capture the normal behaviour specification, as it cannot incorporate variable operational settings that depend on the environment. Further, MUD only supports limited features. Our approach overcomes these limitations by allowing the administrator to define the normal behaviour by choosing combinations from a wider set of features that includes physical layer parameters, values of packet headers, and flow statistics. We developed and implemented a learning-based system that captures and demodulates wireless packets from IoT devices over a period of time, extracts the features specified in the normal behaviour specification, and uses a learning algorithm to create a normal model of each device. Our implementation also enforces these normal models by detecting violations and taking appropriate actions, in terms of ACLs on an Internet Gateway, against the misbehaving devices. Hence, our framework makes the specification tighter and clearer than what is possible with MUD alone, thereby making IoT systems more secure.

Keywords: Internet of Things · Security ·
Manufacturer Usage Description (MUD) · Clustering

1   Introduction

Internet of Things (IoT), defined as an interconnection of things, people, data, and processes meant to achieve some specified business goals, is an important

This material is based upon work supported in whole or in part with funding from the United States Department of Defense (DoD). Any opinions, findings, conclusions, or recommendations expressed in this material are those of the author(s) and do not necessarily reflect the views of any agency or entity of the United States Government.

V. Issarny et al. (Eds.): ICIOT 2019, LNCS 11519, pp. 43–57, 2019.
https://doi.org/10.1007/978-3-030-23357-0_4

emerging technology that is being leveraged heavily by companies. The Business Insider predicts that companies will accelerate their investment in IoT solutions, with the aggregate investment forecasted to be $15 trillion between 2017 and 2025 [29]. Wireless sensor networks (WSN) are a key foundation of IoT solutions, helping things to communicate data to people and processes, and vice versa.

WSNs comprise multiple sensors spread across an area, that measure certain physical parameters of the environment and communicate these measurements wirelessly to a gateway, which in turn forwards it to a control server. WSNs may also "close the loop", i.e. the control server may process these measurements and command some actuators to perform actions to control some physical parameters. Advances in microcontroller, wireless communication, networking, and sensor technologies have made WSNs economical, power-efficient, and easy to setup and maintain. These developments are driving the adoption of WSNs for IoT solutions, for example, in smart power grids, smart water networks, intelligent transportation, health care, industrial process monitoring and control, and smart homes. Aided by technologies like WSNs, the IoT world is growing from 2 billion smart "things" in 2006 to a projected 200 billion by 2020, i.e. around 26 smart "things" for every human being on Earth [17].

As WSNs are becoming more common and the IoT is starting to control important infrastructure, ensuring security in IoT is becoming critical. IoT has deep penetration in manufacturing, healthcare, and business. By 2025, the global worth of IoT technologies is projected to be $6.2 trillion, with the maximum value from health care ($2.5 trillion) and manufacturing ($2.3 trillion) [17]. Aruba Networks also predicted that 87% of the health care organizations would have adopted IoT technologies by 2019 [16]. These numbers illustrate IoT's importance, and also imply that security breaches would have serious consequences for people's lives, industry, and the economy.

Security breaches may happen at the level of the device, in the communication protocols, and/or in the cloud. Current approaches to security are mostly reactive, i.e. software, protocol and chip designers take remedial measures after attackers or researchers discover loopholes. Attackers then again find vulnerabilities in the "fixed" designs, and the cycle continues, like a cat and mouse game that gets increasingly difficult as the complexity of the systems increase. For example, in 2015, two cyber-security experts exploited vulnerabilities in the IoT communication layer and used a man-in-the-middle attack to take control of a Jeep on the freeway, leading to the recall of 1.4 million vehicles. Further, in 2015, a UK based telecom and Internet provider, "Talk Talk", was subject to several security breaches, wherein customers's credit card details were exposed, as they were stored unencrypted in the cloud. This prompted cloud providers to improve their service's security.

IoT devices can be easy targets for attackers due to vulnerabilities in the firmware, weak passwords, open telnet ports, and other loopholes. The situation is aggravated by scale and diversity - while administrators may find it easy to keep a few devices secure, it is more challenging to do so for hundreds and thousands of different types of devices, which may be from different vendors.

Cisco Systems predicts that by 2020 there will be some 50 billion networked devices [2]. As the number of devices grow, more security breaches will follow as security solutions and improvements are not keeping pace [28]. IoT botnets (e.g. Mirai, BrickerBot and Hajime) are commonly used in attacks carried out using IoT devices. These botnets have three major characteristics: their setup is fast and easy, their distribution is rapid, and the deployed malware is difficult to detect [2]. The common solution to thwart botnets has been to use stringent policy rules. Unfortunately, policies have not been expressive enough to handle these security breaches [32]. As the policies depend on user's activity and device features, they tend to become complex and difficult to manage. The policies also vary with the manufacturer, as each manufacturer provides different features to the users.

Securing the network has always been a subservient motive in the industry. In 2018, we saw a significant number of companies updating their privacy policies and terms of services. Due to data breaches in major companies, security and privacy has become one of the primary concerns of both the service providers and the consumers. Owners and providers often do not take basic measures to secure their networks [26]. Most of the major attacks took place because users and providers did not upgrade the kernels or did not change the default password on their network devices [2]. With a simple search on "Shodan", a list of default passwords of every device can be found [12].

Prevention is better than cure, so proactive security measures are needed rather than reactive ones. In this work, we implement a framework that leverages learning techniques and proactively secures IoT devices. The rest of this paper is organized as follows. Section 2 compares our study with related work in the academia and the industry. Section 3 explains our theoretical framework, describing our architecture and our chosen learning technique. Section 4 then details the implementation of our framework. Section 4.3 presents our results and finally, Section 5 concludes our paper.

2   Related Work

IoT devices have a specific purpose, and thus have a small number of predictable traffic flows [31]. This has been harnessed in a positive way by the IETF's Manufacturer Usage Description (MUD) framework. In the MUD framework, the manufacturer of an IoT device specifies the device's intended purpose and communication patterns in a MUD file, which is an instance of a YANG model, serialized in JSON format. This MUD file is stored on the manufacturer's website and can be fetched using a MUD Uniform Resource Locator (URL). The IoT device transmits this MUD URL to the Gateway when the device joins the network. An entity in the network management system, termed the MUD Controller, uses this MUD URL to fetch the MUD file. The MUD Controller then ensures that the IoT device's behaviour and communication is constrained accordingly, for example, by applying access control lists (ACLs) at the Gateway.

The promise of the MUD framework for securing networks and the challenge of integrating it has begun to attract the research community's attention.

YANG can be used to describe the normal models and NETCONF deliver them to devices [11,15,18]. Tools like MUDGEE have been developed for generating MUD files from device traffic traces (PCAPs). MUDdy tool uses the concept of metagraphs to check the validity of the MUD file [23]. MUD policies have been integrated with SDN for IoT intrusion-detection by developing and implementing a system that translates MUD policies to flow rules that can proactively be configured on network switches [22].

Due to the predictability in device behaviour, signature-based machine learning techniques have been employed on network traffic to classify and identify the devices [27]. Machine learning is becoming popular in network and security. Machine learning has been used to successfully identify the source Network Interface Card (NIC) over wireless medium by employing Support Vector Machine (SVM) and k-nearest neighbours (kNN) methods [21]. Various intrusion-detection tools, e.g. OSSEC, Snort, Suricata and Bro, can be used to detect and prevent attacks using rule-based approach. Supervised learning systems can be used for detecting malware by analyzing network traffic using tools like WEKA, which can outperform these intrusion-detection tools [19].

While the MUD framework is an important step in constraining the behaviour of IoT devices and keeping them on a leash, it is still in the draft stage and has its limitations. The YANG model in the latest draft only supports specifying inbound and outbound ACLs, which may not be enough to keep the device on a tight leash. For example, an attacker may hijack devices and overwhelm a gateway by increasing the data rate, while using the prescribed port numbers and still remaining within the defined normal "box". To keep the devices on a tighter leash, the normal behaviour description should consist of multiple smaller "boxes" rather than one big "box", i.e., more features have to be specified, with narrower ranges. In the above case, the data rate calculated over a specified interval of time could be included in the normal behaviour specification. Further, it could be a challenge for the manufacturer to create a MUD file for their device if the intended behaviour depends on operational settings. Consider a temperature sensor that may be configured by an administrator to transmit readings at different intervals, depending on the operational environment. In such cases, the normal behaviour cannot be tightly defined by the manufacturer a priori, as it is set by the operator. Hence, the MUD file may be at best incomplete, or worse, unavailable.

In our work, we overcome these limitations by developing a learning-based system that observes the wireless communications of devices over a period of time and learns a model for the normal behaviour of each device. The system validates the communications of all devices against the corresponding normal models in real time. Deviations from the normal model are used to isolate and block misbehaving devices, before they can they do damage. Hence, because our system learns the normal model, it can augment an incomplete behaviour specification in the MUD file, or substitute a missing one. We provide flexibility in both choosing the features to be included in the normal behaviour specification, and the combination in which the features are used to specify the normal behaviour. This helps our system to specify multiple smaller normal "boxes", giving less leeway to attackers. Further, as our system captures the wireless transmissions of the devices directly off the air, we get access to extra features for defining the normal behaviour, like signal to noise ratio, modulation type and other physical layer information. Therefore, our proposed system can make the normal behaviour specification clearer than that possible using MUD alone, i.e. clearer than MUD.

3   Overview of the Framework Architecture

3.1   System Architecture and Components

Our goal is to design a proactive system that creates normal profiles of IoT devices by observing their wireless transmissions, detects abnormal behaviour, identifies the abnormal device and takes actions against that abnormal device.

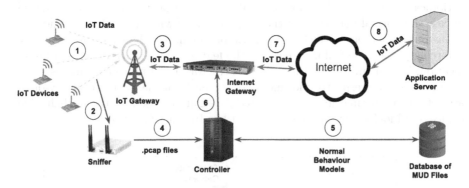

Fig. 1. High level functional blocks of the system's architecture, with arrows indicating directional or bidirectional flow of traffic

Figure 1 shows the functional blocks in our system's architecture. In our framework, IoT Devices, which may be sensors or actuators, transmit their measurements wirelessly to the IoT Gateway or receive actuation signals from the IoT Gateway. These communications are shown by ①. In order to create a normal profile of the devices, their communications have to be captured, decoded and then characterized. We use a Sniffer to eavesdrop on and decode the device's communications as shown by ②. The IoT Gateway demodulates the wireless transmissions of the device and is responsible for forwarding the traffic to the Internet Gateway as shown by ③. The Internet Gateway receives the traffic generated by the sensors via the IoT Gateway and, depending on the actions that are configured on the Internet Gateway, the traffic is then forwarded to the destination, which is the Application Server, ⑧ via the Internet ⑦. All the actions taken by the Controller to thwart the attacks will be implemented on the Internet Gateway. The Sniffer is responsible for capturing and decoding the packets sent or received by the IoT Devices. Packet Captures (pcaps) are generated as an output of the Sniffer and are sent to the Controller for further processing, as shown by ④. The Controller, which is the core of our system and is detailed in Sect. 3.2, receives PCAPs as input and is responsible for extracting relevant features, creating a normal model ⑤ and enforcing the generated model on the Internet Gateway ⑥. The functions of the Controller are detailed in Sect. 3.2.

3.2 Learning Technique

As mentioned above, the Controller is the core of our system's architecture. A simplified block diagram of the Controller is shown in Fig. 2. The feature extractor module receives pcaps from the Sniffer and extracts the desired features. During the learning phase, the features are stored for a duration of time, termed the "learning interval", and then these stored features processed by the learning module to create the normal models of the devices. These normal models are stored as MUD files in the database. The Controller learns the normal models periodically after every learning interval to ensure that the models are updated in case the normal behaviour of the devices change with time. Once the normal behaviour models have been learnt, the Enforcer enforces these models during the enforcing phase. The Enforcer receives the features of the each device's communication, in real time, from the feature extractor. The Enforcer compares these features with the respective normal models read from the database. If any deviation from the normal model is detected, the Enforcer isolates the misbehaving device and blocks it by applying ACLs at the Internet Gateway.

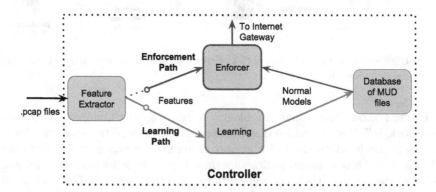

Fig. 2. A simplified version of the Controller, illustrating its main functions - learning the normal model, storing the model into a database, and enforcing the model.

Various learning methods can be used to model the normal behaviour of the device, and these can be categorized into supervised learning and unsupervised learning. Among these methods, it has been shown that performance of unsupervised learning is not affected by unknown characteristics or information and is similar to the performance of the supervised learning [24]. The disadvantage of using supervised methods for characteristics detection is that the labelling procedure of training data is expensive in terms of computation and is time consuming. The unsupervised anomaly detection approach overcomes this problem by making use of data-clustering algorithms, which make no assumptions about the labels or classes of the pattern. Data is grouped such that patterns within the same groups are more similar to each other than they are to patterns belonging to different groups. Since IoT devices have completely different patterns for different features, unsupervised learning using clustering is a good fit.

Among different clustering techniques, hierarchical clustering is preferable when the number of clusters is not known a priori, as it is both more flexible and has fewer assumptions about the distribution of the underlying data. Clustering algorithms like k-means need a criterion to define a correct or acceptable number of clusters, but such information may not be available in some systems [20]. Though hierarchical clustering can be computationally more expensive, it is robust with respect to choice of number of clusters, and can detect outliers (suspicious data points). Hierarchical clustering is also easy to implement, and it is easy to interpret its the results [30]. Hence, a hierarchical clustering learning algorithm is preferable for classifying the behaviour of IoT devices in WSNs, as the number of normal clusters are not known a priori.

Hierarchical clustering starts by treating each data point as a separate cluster. At each step, a distance metric is used to identify the two closest clusters, and these clusters are merged to a single cluster. This continues until all the clusters are merged together. The distance between the two clusters, merged at a given step of the hierarchical clustering algorithm, is termed the "inter-cluster distance". The output of the hierarchical clustering is a dendrogram, which is a tree structure showing the hierarchical relationship between clusters, with cluster numbers on the X-axis and inter-cluster distance on the Y-axis. To obtain a group of clusters, the dendrogram can be "cut" by a horizontal line, corresponding to a specific inter-cluster distance, and a specific cluster merging step.

After performing hierarchical clustering, the next step is to find the best location of this horizontal line, to cut the dendrogram thus obtained, such that the resultant cluster partition is the optimum. The increase in inter-cluster distance between successive cluster merging steps, which we denote by $\delta_{interClusterDistance}$, can be used to guide this search. A large value of $\delta_{interClusterDistance}$ at a merging step indicates that the merged clusters are dissimilar and probably belong to different groups. Hence, the candidate locations to cut the dendrogram are those where the next cluster merging step leads to a large value of $\delta_{interClusterDistance}$. To choose the best location among all these candidates, a metric is needed to measure the "quality" of the corresponding clustering results. We use the silhouette analysis technique as the metric. This technique computes a metric for each data point, termed the "silhouette score", which is a measure of how well that data point lies within its cluster.

The silhouette score for a data point x is calculated as follows:

$$s(x) = \frac{\bar{d}_{c'}(x) - \bar{d}_c(x)}{max\{\bar{d}_{c'}(x), \bar{d}_c(x)\}},$$

where $\bar{d}_c(x)$ is the average distance between x and all other datapoints within the same cluster, and $\bar{d}_{c'}(x)$ is the smallest average distance between x to all points in any other cluster that does not have x as a member.

The silhouette score ranges from -1 to $+1$, and can be averaged over all the data points to obtain a mean silhouette score. Higher values of the mean silhouette score indicate that the cluster partition is appropriate, while lower values indicate that the partition may have too many, or too few clusters. Among all the candidate clustering results described previously, the optimum is chosen such that it yields the highest mean silhouette score. This learning algorithm is detailed in Sect. 4.2. In this way, based on these optimum clusters obtained with hierarchical clustering and silhouette analysis, normal models are learned for classifying the behaviour of IoT devices.

4   Testbed Implementation, Experiments and Results

To put theory to practice, a testbed was implemented, comprising all the components of the theoretical framework discussed above: a wireless sensor network, a Sniffer that eavesdrops on and decodes all wireless transmissions, and a Controller that supervises the devices. To enable the research and academic community to build on this work, this testbed has been open-sourced [13,14]. In this section, we describe this testbed and present the results of experiments conducted using it.

4.1   System Components

LoRa [7] and LoRaWAN [1], which are predicted to be the dominant physical and medium access control protocols for private LPWANs [8], were chosen to demonstrate the capabilities of our framework and its potential to be used in real life IoT networks. Other IoT communication technologies like SigFox, Narrowband IoT (NB-IoT), and LTE CAT 1, can also be supported over our testbed, with compatible devices, a compatible gateway, and by updating the Sniffer to demodulate and decode the respective communication protocols. As depicted in Fig. 3, Multitech mDot [10] devices were chosen as the programmable IoT Devices, a Multitech Conduit LoRa Gateway [9] as the LoRaWAN Gateway, and an Ettus USRP B210 [3], controlled by the GNU Radio toolkit, as the Sniffer. Linux containers [6], managed using LXD, were used to emulate the IoT Gateway, Application Server and the Controller. An alternative to decoding transmissions "off the air", is to capture packets "on the wire", at the interface of the Gateway towards the IoT Devices, and forward these packets to the Controller.

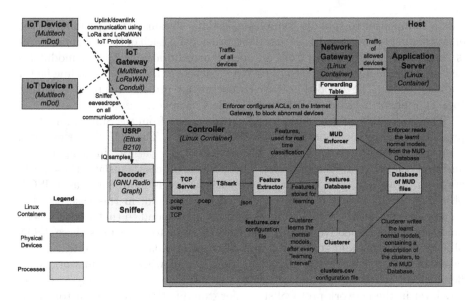

Fig. 3. Implementation diagram depicting the mapping of the theoretical framework components to actual devices, Linux containers and processes.

The mDots use LoRaWAN's Over the Air Authentication (OTAA) scheme to the join the LoRaWAN Gateway. This scheme requires the mDots to be setup with certain keys. This configuration was performed using MBed's online compiler. To emulate normal and abnormal behaviour, the mDot was also programmed to transmit payloads of desired length, and at desired intervals of time. The mDots were configured to use the US 902–928 MHz industrial, scientific and medical (ISM) band, and to operate in hybrid mode in sub-band 1. Therefore, the mDots hopped in frequency between one of eight channels spaced at intervals of 200 kHz from 902.3 MHz to 903.9 MHz when transmitting with 125 MHz bandwidth, and will transmit at 903 MHz when using 500 MHz bandwidth.

The transmissions of the mDot are decoded by the Multitech LoRaWAN Gateway and encapsulated in TCP datagrams with the destination IP being the interface of the Application Server container connected to the Internet Gateway container. These datagrams are then forwarded to the Internet Gateway, whose forwarding table is configured to forward these packets out on the correct interface. These packets are received and logged by a TCP server at the Application Server container.

The wireless transmissions of the mDot devices are captured off the air and sampled by the USRP, connected to a laptop via a USB 3.0 cable, and controlled by a GNU-Radio flow graph running on that laptop. The USRP is configured to receive at a center frequency of 914.9 MHz and sample at 30 MHz, allowing it to capture all transmissions from approximately 900 MHz to 930 MHz. The IQ samples generated by the USRP are transmitted over the USB cable to the laptop, where they are processed by the flow graph in real time. This flow graph uses a channelizer to split the samples into eight streams, corresponding to the eight channels of sub-band 1, as described previously. Each of these eight streams is then processed by blocks from an open-source library [4], that demodulates and decodes the IQ samples into LoRaWAN packets at a specific spreading factor and bandwidth. The decoded LoRaWAN packets are presented in pcap [5] format to a TCP client, which forwards them to the Controller.

The Controller receives and processes the packets from the Sniffer, and comprises multiple sub-components as illustrated in Fig. 3. The TCP Server receives, from the Sniffer, the packets sent by the devices or the gateway, in .pcap format, and feeds them to a T-Shark process. The T-Shark process translates these packets from .pcap into .json format, where each packet is represented as a JSON object. A JSON object is a set of key value pairs, and, in this case, the key value pairs of a packet's JSON object directly correspond to that packet's pcap fields and their respective values. The feature extractor consumes these JSON objects, extracting and storing relevant features in a database. The features to be extracted are specified in a configuration file, allowing the framework to be flexible and adapt to different protocols. These features may be any header of any layer in the network protocol stack, for example the spreading factor in the LoRa PHY header, or may be statistics calculated from the flow, for example the inter-arrival time. In this way, each packet, transmitted or received by an IoT device, is eventually represented by a set of features, termed as "packet-features". Furthermore, the feature extractor can identify and distinguish between different devices based on certain field(s) in the packet. This enables the feature extractor to store features of each device separately, enabling the framework to learn a normal behaviour model for each individual device. For the LoRaWAN protocol, the "device address" field in the MAC header is used to uniquely identify a device within a LoRaWAN network. This database of features, gathered over a period of time, is used as a training dataset by the Clusterer to create a model for the normal behaviour of each IoT device. Once the normal behaviour models have been learnt, the Controller can start classifying packets in real time, i.e., the feature extractor forwards a packet's features and the device identity to the Enforcer, which validates the features against that device's normal model, as learnt by Clusterer and saved in the database. The learning and classification functions, performed by the Clusterer and the Enforcer respectively, are detailed in the following subsection.

4.2 Learning

The proposed framework enables the administrator to tightly characterize the IoT devices by allowing her to influence the number and the dimensions of the normal "boxes". This influence is exerted by specifying multiple different combinations of features in a configuration file, which is read by the Clusterer. The Clusterer generates normal clusters for each specified feature combination, by processing the features stored in the database. After the features from the captured packets are stored in the database for the learning interval, the Clusterer learns normal behaviour models from these stored features. To better understand the algorithm, we step through it using an example. Assume that the administrator has specified two feature combinations in the configuration file, for a LoRaWAN-compliant GPS sensor: "packet length, inter-arrival time" and "frequency". Assume that, normally, the GPS sensor sends packets of length 45 bytes, at intervals of 60 s, and is configured to operate in US sub-band 1. Assume that, during the learning interval, the GPS sensor loses GPS lock a few times and as a result, for some packets, the inter-arrival time is much higher than 60 s. The Clusterer fetches all "packet-features", for this GPS sensor, from the features database. For the first feature combination, "packet length, inter-arrival time", after extracting the "packet length" and "inter-arrival" fields from each "packet-feature", the Clusterer standardizes these two features. As our cluster analysis algorithm uses Euclidean distance to measure the separation between observations and clusters, standardization is needed to prevent features that are on a larger scale than others, from exerting a stronger influence on the distance measurements and clustering results. For example, measuring the inter-arrival time in milliseconds instead of seconds may change the clustering results. Further, when detecting abnormalities, a deviation in packet length of 10 bytes is more significant than a deviation in inter-arrival time of 10 ms. Hence, the features are standardized, and the recommended approach of using absolute deviation around the mean to detect outliers, rather than using standard deviation, is followed [25]. These standardized feature values, arranged in a matrix, are the input to the hierarchical clustering algorithm. As described in Sect. 3, the optimum clusters are obtained by evaluating different clustering results of the hierarchical clustering algorithm using silhouette analysis. In this case, the optimal clustering would comprise two clusters - one corresponding to the specified behaviour of the sensor, and another corresponding to the observations immediately following the GPS loss. The centroids of these normal clusters represent the normal values for this feature combination, and are added to the normal behaviour specification. In this case, depending on how accurately the GPS sensor follows its specifications, the centroid of the first normal cluster is a point with inter-arrival time approximately 60 s, and packet length approximately 45 bytes, and that of the second normal cluster is a point with packet length approximately 45 bytes, and inter-arrival time greater than 60 s, depending on the delay in obtaining a GPS lock. For the next feature combination, "frequency", the Clusterer identifies eight normal clusters, corresponding to the eight channels in US sub-band 1. The centroids of these clusters, corresponding to the center frequencies of these eight channels, are added to the normal behaviour specification. Hence, in effect, the normal behaviour specification specifies that, for the observed behaviour to be considered normal, it should lie in at least one of the above 11 normal clusters.

Once this normal behaviour model has been learnt, it is enforced by the Enforcer, which validated the captured packets against all the normal clusters of all the specified feature combinations. For a given feature combination, a packet that falls outside any of the corresponding normal clusters is marked as abnormal. For instance, if an attacker hijacks the GPS sensor and starts sending packets frequently, at intervals of 10 s, then the second packet transmitted by the hijacked sensor will have an abnormal inter-arrival time. This packet will fall outside the two normal clusters defined for the combination of packet length and inter-arrival time. Hence, the GPS sensor's behaviour will be classified as abnormal, and that sensor will be blocked by the Enforcer by applying appropriate ACLs at the Gateway.

Table 1. Parameters of the experimental setup

Parameter	Value
Hardware	Ettus USRP B210 connected to a laptop via a USB 3.0 cable as the Sniffer, MultiConnect mDots as the IoT Devices and Multitech Conduit as the LoRaWAN Gateway
Software	GNU Radio and gr-lora in the Sniffer for decoding packets, LXD to manage linux containers, TShark for converting pcaps to json format, sklearn python library for clustering, and pyang python library for parsing and writing yang files
"Normal" pairs of (inter-arrival time, framelength)	(10–11 s, 90 or 91 bytes), (21–23 s, 99 bytes)
"Abnormal" pairs of (inter-arrival time, framelength)	(21–23 s, 99 bytes), (11 s, 98 bytes), (15 s, 94 bytes), (16 s, 97 bytes), (20 s, 92 bytes)
mDot operation mode	Hybrid mode in US sub-band 1 (902–928 MHz)
LoRaWAN uplink spreading factor	8
LoRaWAN uplink bandwidth	500 kHz
LoRaWAN downlink bandwidth	500 kHz
USRP center frequency	914.9 MHz
USRP sampling rate	30 MHz

4.3   Experiments and Results

The testbed described above was used to learn normal behaviour models for two mDots. The mDots were configured to use a spreading factor of 8 and a bandwidth of 500 kHz for their uplink transmissions. In their normal mode, the mDots were programmed to alternatively transmit smaller frames with shorter inter-arrival times, and larger frames with larger inter-arrival times, as specified in Table 1. A training database was created by capturing and decoding frames from the mDots for a duration of eight hours. Then, the Clusterer learnt the

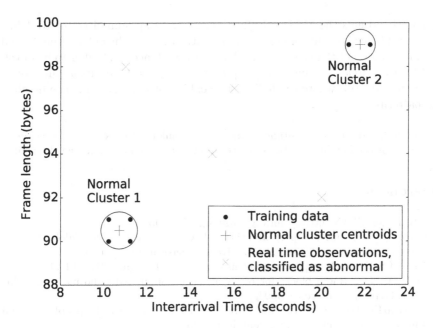

Fig. 4. An illustration of how the normal model is learnt and enforced. The normal model is learnt by clustering the training data, which results in two normal clusters. Real time observations are then classified as normal or abnormal, based on their distance from the centroids of the two normal clusters.

normal model by clustering using the feature combination of "inter-arrival time and frame length", the results of which are shown in Fig. 4.

Abnormal behaviour was emulated by commanding an mDot, via a downlink message, to change the framelength and interval-arrival time to any of the abnormal values listed in Table 1. The resulting observations are depicted by "crosses" in Fig. 4. As these points lie outside the normal clusters, the Enforcer classified the observations as abnormal, and installed ACLs at the IoT Gateway to drop all traffic from the corresponding mDot. The IETF's MUD framework does not currently support specifying the normal behaviour in terms of combinations of inter-arrival time and framelength, with multiple "normal" pairs. Hence, it would not be able to detect this abnormal behaviour. In this way, our framework extends the MUD specification.

5   Conclusion

A framework for enhancing security in IoT WSNs, by learning and enforcing normal behaviour models for IoT devices, was designed, implemented, and demonstrated on a testbed based on LoRaWAN technology. An experiment was conducted to demonstrate the ability of our framework to learn the normal behaviour model, detect abnormal behaviour and thwart potential attacks. This framework extends the MUD specification, allowing an administrator to define the normal behaviour model flexibly and tightly, and thereby enforce the desired level of security in her IoT solutions. The framework needs a Sniffer to be developed for the wireless communication protocol being used, and its application is limited to scenarios where the IoT devices exhibit strong "normal" communication patterns.

Acknowledgements. The authors would like to thank the United States Department of Defense for the funding and the support, and Signalscape for developing the Sniffer.

References

1. About LoRaWAN. https://lora-alliance.org/about-lorawan
2. Cisco's Cybersecurity Report 2017. https://www.cisco.com/c/dam/global/es_mx/solutions/security/pdf/cisco-2017-midyear-cybersecurity-report.pdf
3. Ettus USRP B210. https://www.ettus.com/product/details/UB210-KIT
4. gr-Lora: GNU Radio blocks for receiving LoRa modulated radio messages using SDR. https://github.com/rpp0/gr-lora
5. Libpcap File Format. https://wiki.wireshark.org/Development/LibpcapFileFormat
6. Linux containers. https://linuxcontainers.org/
7. LoRa Modulation Basics, by Semtech. https://www.semtech.com/uploads/documents/an1200.22.pdf
8. LPWAN Market Report 2018–2023, by IoT Analytics. https://iot-analytics.com/lpwan-market-report-2018-2023-new-report/
9. Multitech Conduit Gateway. https://www.multitech.com/brands/multiconnect-conduit
10. Multitech mDot. https://www.multitech.com/brands/multiconnect-mdot
11. NETCONF RFC 6241. https://datatracker.ietf.org/doc/rfc6241/
12. Shodan's search engine for devices connected to the Internet. https://www.shodan.io/
13. Source code for the "Clearer Than Mud" framework, in gzip format. https://research.ece.ncsu.edu/wireless/MadeInWALAN/ClearerThanMUD/ClearerThanMUDFramework.tar.gz
14. Source code for the "Clearer Than Mud" framework, in zip format. https://research.ece.ncsu.edu/wireless/MadeInWALAN/ClearerThanMUD/ClearerThanMUDFramework.zip
15. YANG RFC 7950. https://datatracker.ietf.org/doc/rfc7950/
16. State of IoT, Healthcare, a study by Aruba Networks, February 2017. https://www.arubanetworks.com/assets/infographic/Aruba_IoT_Healthcare_Infographic.pdf
17. A Guide to the Internet of Things, January 2018. https://www.intel.com/content/www/us/en/internet-of-things/infographics/guide-to-iot.html
18. Manufacturer Usage Description Specification, June 2018. https://datatracker.ietf.org/doc/draft-ietf-opsawg-mud/
19. Bekerman, D., Shapira, B., Rokach, L., Bar, A.: Unknown malware detection using network traffic classification. In: 2015 IEEE Conference on Communications and Network Security (CNS), pp. 134–142. IEEE (2015)
20. Bharti, K., Shukla, S., Jain, S.: Intrusion detection using unsupervised learning. Int. J. Comput. Sci. Eng. **2**(5), 1865 (2010)

21. Brik, V., Banerjee, S., Gruteser, M., Oh, S.: Wireless device identification with radiometric signatures. In: Proceedings of the 14th ACM International Conference on Mobile Computing and Networking, pp. 116–127. ACM (2008)
22. Hamza, A., Gharakheili, H.H., Sivaraman, V.: Combining mud policies with SDN for IoT intrusion detection. In: Proceedings of the 2018 Workshop on IoT Security and Privacy, pp. 1–7. ACM (2018)
23. Hamza, A., Ranathunga, D., Gharakheili, H.H., Roughan, M., Sivaraman, V.: Clear as MUD: generating, validating and applying IoT behavioral profiles. In: Proceedings of the 2018 Workshop on IoT Security and Privacy, pp. 8–14. ACM (2018)
24. Laskov, P., Düssel, P., Schäfer, C., Rieck, K.: Learning intrusion detection: supervised or unsupervised? In: Roli, F., Vitulano, S. (eds.) ICIAP 2005. LNCS, vol. 3617, pp. 50–57. Springer, Heidelberg (2005). https://doi.org/10.1007/11553595_6
25. Leys, C., Ley, C., Klein, O., Bernard, P., Licata, L.: Detecting outliers: do not use standard deviation around the mean, use absolute deviation around the median. J. Exp. Soc. Psychol. **49**(4), 764–766 (2013)
26. Loi, F., Sivanathan, A., Gharakheili, H.H., Radford, A., Sivaraman, V.: Systematically evaluating security and privacy for consumer IoT devices. In: Proceedings of the 2017 Workshop on Internet of Things Security and Privacy, pp. 1–6. ACM (2017)
27. Meidan, Y., et al.: ProfilIoT: a machine learning approach for IoT device identification based on network traffic analysis. In: Proceedings of the Symposium on Applied Computing, pp. 506–509. ACM (2017)
28. Mendez, D.M., Papapanagiotou, I., Yang, B.: Internet of Things: survey on security and privacy. arXiv preprint arXiv:1707.01879 (2017)
29. Newman, P.: The Internet of Things Report, July 2018. https://www.businessinsider.com/internet-of-things-report
30. Nieves, J.F., Jiao, Y.C.: Data clustering for anomaly detection in network intrusion detection. Research Alliance in Math and Science, pp. 1–12 (2009)
31. Sivanathan, A., et al.: Characterizing and classifying IoT traffic in smart cities and campuses. In: 2017 IEEE Conference on Computer Communications Workshops (INFOCOM WKSHPS), pp. 559–564. IEEE (2017)
32. Yu, T., Sekar, V., Seshan, S., Agarwal, Y., Xu, C.: Handling a trillion (unfixable) flaws on a billion devices: rethinking network security for the internet-of-things. In: Proceedings of the 14th ACM Workshop on Hot Topics in Networks, p. 5. ACM (2015)

A WS-Agreement Based SLA Ontology
for IoT Services

Fan Li$^{(\boxtimes)}$ (iD), Christian Cabrera$^{(\boxtimes)}$ (iD), and Siobhán Clarke$^{(\boxtimes)}$ (iD)

Trinity College Dublin, College Green, Dublin, Ireland
{fali,cabrerac,Siobhan.Clarke}@scss.tcd.ie

Abstract. In the Internet of Things (IoT), billions of physical devices, distributed over a large geographic area, provide a near real-time state of the world. These devices' capabilities can be abstracted as IoT services and delivered to users in a demand-driven way. In such a dynamic large-scale environment, a service provider who supports a service level agreement (SLA) can have a comprehensive competitive edge in terms of service quality management, service customization, optimized resource allocation, and trustworthiness. However, there is no consistent way of drafting an SLA with respect to describing heterogeneous IoT services, which obstructs automatic service selection, SLA negotiation, and SLA monitoring. In this paper, we propose an ontology, WIoT-SLA, to achieve semantic interoperability. We combine IoT service properties with two prominent web service SLA specifications: WS-Agreement and WSLA, to take advantage of their complementary features. This ontology is used to formalize the SLAs and SLA negotiation offers, which further facilitates the service selection and automatic SLA negotiation. It can also be used by a monitoring engine to detect SLA violations by providing the semantics of service level objectives (SLOs) and quality metrics. To evaluate our work, a prototype is implemented to demonstrate its feasibility and efficiency.

Keywords: Internet of Things · SLA · Service level management · SLA ontology

1   Introduction

The Internet of Things (IoT) is an ambient smart environment where a large number of interconnected physical objects interact with the physical world, providing a near real-time state of the environment. Each device's functionalities can be abstracted as an IoT service provided through a well-defined interface in a homogeneous way [22]. For mission-critical IoT applications, "best effort" services are not sufficient [21]. In many service provisioning needs, SLAs are widely used as a contract to provide a certain level of control to a consumer

Supported by Science Foundation Ireland (SFI) under the project SURF - grant 13/IA/1885.

V. Issarny et al. (Eds.): ICIOT 2019, LNCS 11519, pp. 58–72, 2019.
https://doi.org/10.1007/978-3-030-23357-0_5

and deliver requested services with pre-negotiated quality of service (QoS). In SLAs, the obligations and guarantees of involved parties are specified in the form of Service Level Objectives (SLOs), which are evaluated using measurable data [16].

To our best knowledge, SLA management in IoT platforms is still in a preliminary stage [17]. However, providing a precise SLA specification for IoT services would enable a better QoS-aware service management [12]. For example, the varying syntax of different SLAs obstructs automatic service matching and SLA negotiation in large-scale electronic markets. Consumers or third-party audit agents struggle to detect SLA violations unless they understand the SLA document. To achieve semantic interoperability and reduce the ambiguity in automating negotiation and monitoring activities, the common solution is to create SLA ontologies [19]. Current SLAs languages for cloud services and web services do not capture characteristics of IoT services. How to draft SLAs with respect to describing IoT services abstracted from the large, distributed and heterogeneous sources is still a problem.

In light of this gap, this paper presents an ontology for automatic SLA management in an IoT environment: WIoT-SLA. This ontology combines two of the most commonly-used web service SLA specifications: WS-Agreement [1] and WSLA [16]. These languages have complementary features: WS-Agreement has a well-structured schema with supports for the extension of new domain-specific elements and SLA negotiation, while WSLA defines metric descriptions of SLA parameters. This paper extend the WS-Agreement schema with a set of general IoT domain-specific concepts, which enables constraint-based SLA modeling for automatic service selection, SLA negotiation and SLA creation.

The reminder of the paper is organized as follows: Sect. 2 summarizes related work. Section 3 describes the ontology-based SLA management for IoT services. Section 4 proposes the contextual SLA ontology. Section 5 presents the SLA template match-making algorithm for optimized candidate service selection. Section 6 details the experimental setup and evaluation results and Sect. 7 concludes the paper with a discussion about future research directions.

2   Related Work

SLA specification languages are central to the definition of an SLA contract. There have been significant works in defining SLA languages for web services and cloud services. IBM published the Web Service Level Agreement (WSLA), which provides a specification for the definition and monitoring of SLAs within a web service environment [16]. WS-Agreement is another XML-based web service SLA specification defined by Open Grid Forum (OGF) [1]. Compared to WSLA, it defines a decoupled negotiation layer on top of the agreement layer for bilateral multi-round negotiation: WS-Agreement Negotiation [26]. Inspired by WS-Agreement, Uriarte *et al.* proposed an SLA language for the cloud computing domain. They predefined a set of metrics for Infrastructure-as-a-Service and adopted a denotational semantics [24]. To be decoupled from the XML-schema, the SLA@SOI project proposed an abstract SLA syntax named SLA*

[13] to automate the cloud SLA life cycle. Based on WSLA and SLA*, CSLA was proposed to address SLA violations in cloud computing [14], which supports cloud elasticity management such as the QoS or functionality degradation.

Compared to web services and cloud services, SLA specification targeting IoT services is very limited [17]. Although Gaillard et al. [9] extended the WSLA specification with device information to describe network performance for WSN operators, it focused on modeling the SLAs on the device layer instead of the service layer, while service consumers may be additionally interested in service-oriented aspects rather than just the concrete device information. Current research has developed a number of ontologies to model sensors and sensor observations. The SSN ontology [7] is a high-level model to describe devices' measurement capabilities and related attributes, which is further extended by OpenIoT [20] and IoT-Lite [2] to define sensors, measurements, and locations. The SENSEI project [25] models *Real World Entities* as resources, which are described by a semantic ontology including resource type, location, temporal availability, semantic operation description (e.g., input, output, pre-conditions, post-conditions), observation area, quality, and cost.

Several IoT middlewares also proposed their QoS metrics. For example, OpenIoT defines a set of utility metrics for different IoT layers to manage QoS, which includes energy consumption, delay, bandwidth, latency, etc [5]. The CityPulse project listed the quality categories that are used to assess the quality of observations made in the real world, and summarized the quality parameters with corresponding measurement units and value ranges [23]. However, as far as we know, these QoS metrics have not been integrated into the SLA schema for IoT services.

3   Ontology-Based SLA Management

From the European Commission report on recent cloud computing projects that cover SLAs, the SLA lifecycle meta-model consists of six main phases [15]: **Service use**, which reflects the information on service usage by a consumer. **Service modeling**, which deals with the service design and analysis issues, such as estimating performance and instantiating service parameters. **SLA template definition**, which creates SLA templates by analyzing the business objectives. **SLA instantiation**, which covers various processes including attributes mapping and translation, provider discovery, and dynamic SLA (re-)negotiation. **SLA enforcement**, which aims to verify the reliability of pre-negotiated QoS parameters during the service provisioning time by adopting a QoS monitoring mechanism. **SLA conclusion**, which handles the termination of signed SLAs according to pre-defined accounting and billing mechanisms. If an SLA is terminated as a violated agreement or is predicted to be violated by the QoS monitor, SLA renegotiation may be conducted as a corrective action to maintain service continuity.

The lifecycle meta-model briefly describes how to create and manage SLA-supported services. Since the IoT is a large-scale environment where multiple

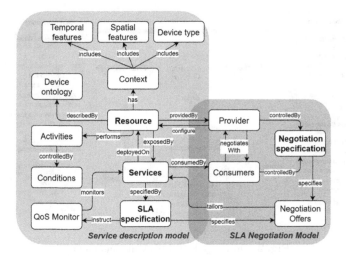

Fig. 1. Upper ontology of IoT SLA core concepts

services offering the same or similar functionalities are distributed in different locations, human intervention may not be feasible to manage services and SLAs. We assume a middleware can be deployed in different IoT gateways, which works in a distributed manner to provide the necessary functionalities such as service selection, SLA negotiation, and QoS monitoring. The service providers outline the functionalities of their SLA-supported services with default values in the form of SLA templates (SLAT) and register them to gateways so that their offerings can be discovered when requests are received by gateways from consumers. Figure 1 shows the upper ontology that describes the relations between the domain-specific core concepts of IoT services. To automate the SLA lifecycle in the IoT environment, a common global knowledge of SLAs is needed to make SLAs reciprocally understandable. This uniform SLA ontology not only allows providers to express their offerings in a standardized way but also helps gateways dynamically adjust the negotiation and monitoring mechanisms based on the metrics, constraints, and conditions defined in the SLAs. Figure 2 presents our ontology-based SLA management model: (i) SLA ontology generalizes the semantics of SLA specification and negotiation specification; (ii) The dynamic SLA negotiation and SLA creation can be performed according to the negotiation context, creation constraints and validation rules specified in the SLAT; (iii) The automatic monitoring can be conducted according to the assessment information (e.g. negotiated guarantees, measurement metrics and assessment schedulers) specified in the SLA; (iv) The service adaptation (i.e., SLA renegotiation) and accounting mechanisms can be triggered by monitored results.

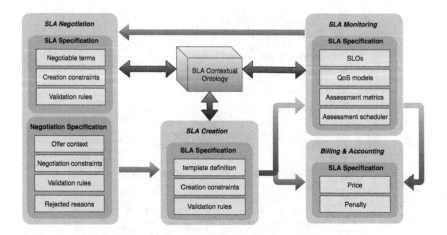

Fig. 2. Ontology-based SLA management

4   SLA Contextual Ontology

The SLA specification defines the standard format of an agreement, which requires a non-ambiguous description of services. The key requirements of defining an SLA schema in the IoT environment are simplicity, reusability, readability and efficiency [18]. In other words, the SLA ontology should contain all the necessary information for automatic SLA management but in the meanwhile, remain as simple as possible. In IoT, three well-accepted concepts are the entity, resource and service [2]. The semantic models of these concepts are associated with each other by attributes such as location, domain information, physical concept and observations. Since an end user may focus more on the service-oriented aspects rather than the physical sensor information described by a sensor ontology, it is useful to merge the important attributes of the entity model and resource model to the service model, and provide a uniform SLA ontology for IoT services.

We built an SLA ontology, called WIoT-SLA, based on an extendable web service SLA specification WS-Agreement (WSAG) [1], which supports for SLA negotiation and widely used in cloud computing projects [15]. We formalized the structure of WIoT-SLA by extending WSAG with IoT domain-specific concepts to improve the readability and efficient traversability of SLA and SLAT. The steps to achieve this were: (i) We linked the domain knowledge relating to sensing, actuating and processing tasks to real-world resources, which enables more flexible and scalable solutions for different IoT application tasks (Sect. 4.1: *Service Description Term*). (ii) We proposed a high-level abstraction of sensing service configuration properties, enabling applications to avoid complex details about devices (e.g., Fig. 5). (iii) We defined the syntax of guarantees and QoS metrics to facilitate SLA monitoring (Sect. 4.1: *Service Property*). (iv) We extended the WSAG template schema to solve the template synchronization problem and reduce the message payload during SLA negotiation (Sect. 4.1: *SLA Template Structure*). (v) We formalized the structure of negotiation offers by extending the WS-Agreement Negotiation specification (WSAG-Negotiation) with offer validation rules and rejected reasons to avoid invalid interactions (Sect. 4.2).

4.1 SLA Description Ontology

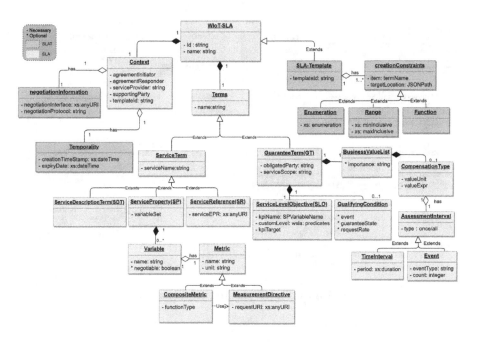

Fig. 3. WIoT-SLA structure

The structure of WIoT-SLA comprises two parts (shown in green on Fig. 3): agreement context (i.e., party information, expiry date, agreement template identifier, etc.) and terms. Services are described by *terms*, which consists of *service description term* (SDT), *service property* (SP), *service reference* (SR), and *guarantee term* (GT). SDT is the fundamental component of an SLA, which describes the functionality that will be delivered by the service. SP is used to define the measurable and exposed QoS properties associated with the service. SR (optional) lists the references point to the service (e.g., a WSDL document or a restful web service interface). GT defines the assurance of SP variables in the form of SLOs, which specifies a customized quality level that is guaranteed by the obligated party. The business objectives associated with an SLO are defined in business value list, which includes the compensation type (i.e., price and penalty) and possibly, the importance factor. The latter would be useful for SLA negotiation if the tradeoff negotiation tactic (i.e. the concession rate can be made based on the weight of each SLO) is adopted. The compensation type specifies the consequence of SLA fulfillment, which is associated with an assessment interval describing how to measure the SLA violation for monitors (e.g., periodic schedule or the number of events that has occurred).

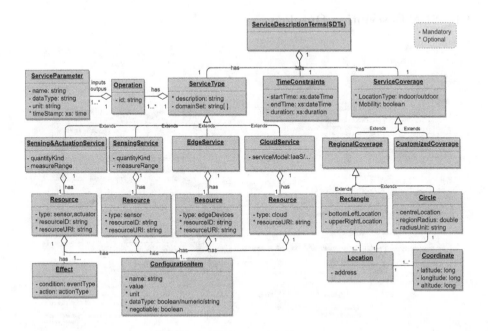

Fig. 4. Service description terms

Service Description Term. Figure 4 shows the ontology of service description terms in WIoT-SLA, which consists of three parts: time constraints, service coverage, and service type. **Time constraints** specifies the actual service provisioning time, which is different from the temporality in an SLAT. **Service coverage** specifies the spatial features of the service (e.g., the observation area of sensors). We pre-defined the rectangle area and circle area for regional coverage. The concrete location can be defined with an address ontology or the geographic coordinate.

Service type generalizes a service's functionality with domain information, operation, service parameters (i.e., input and output) and configurable features. In IoT, the service type can be clustered as a sensing service (e.g., temperature sensing), a sensing and actuation service (e.g., trigger the alarm when detected hazard gas concentration greater than a threshold), an edge service (e.g., a data dispatch service that collects data from sensors and publish verified data to subscribed services) and cloud service (e.g., data storage and data processing service that analyzing historical data and predict abnormalities) based on the

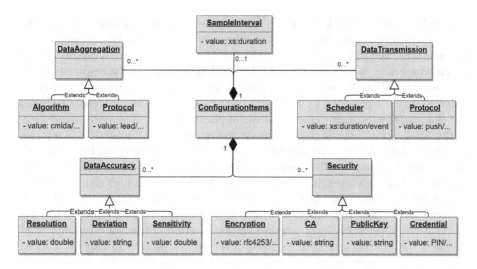

Fig. 5. An example of configuration items (sensing service)

deployed resources. For instance, quality kind can be used to describe the real-world property observed by the sensors, but a sensing and actuation service may have an "effect" attribute describing an event or an action when the pre-defined condition is met. Each resource type is associated with one or more configuration items, which specifies the service's functional features, such as the sample rate for sensing services, data reporting rate for edge services or memory capacity for cloud services. The configuration item is defined with a name, a value, and data type (i.e., boolean, numeric and string) of the value. Figure 5 outlined a set of general configuration items for sensing services, including data accuracy, security, sample rate, data aggregation, and data transmission.

Service Property. In WIoT-SLA, SP variables are defined as the dynamic QoS features (i.e., values are affected by devices' status and run-time environment) that can be monitored by a measurement party. Each SP variable is described by a name, which is further used in expressing SLO in GTs (i.e., *KPIName* in SLO), and the customized metrics specifying its measurement unit. Different from cloud computing and web services, the QoS model in the IoT context needs to consider the complexity introduced by the layered architecture of IoT applications [8]. From bottom to top, the architecture is composed of a perception layer, network layer, service layer, and application layer. In the **perception layer**, a heterogeneous set of devices sample the state of the physical world with different capabilities and constraints. Quality metrics for a perception layer include data correctness, data completeness, transmission speed, energy consumption, price, etc [23]. The **network layer** comprises the network infrastructures on which the IoT platform is based. Quality metrics for the network layer focus on the performance of data transmissions, such as network delay, bandwidth, packet loss, and network jitter [6]. The **service layer** processes information received from the lower layer and provides services such as data storage, data management, and data analysis. *CLOUDQUAL* is an example of a quality model for cloud services, which defines usability, availability, reliability, responsiveness, security, and elasticity as quality dimensions [27]. In the **application layer**, different services provided by the lower layer can be composed together to fulfill the domain-specific requirements of an application task. The end-to-end QoS of the application layer is dependent on the aggregated or nested QoS metrics across the lower layers. For instance, a fire detection application has stringent QoS demands on availability, responsiveness and accuracy, which constrains the quality level of each layer, such as good quality sensors with high data precision, adjustable sampling rate, fast transmission speed, available networks with low latency, and a high reliability for the data processing service. Since achieving SLOs at the application layer requires the satisfaction of the SLOs of lower level services, the guarantee states[1] of lower-level service properties can be used as a precondition under which the application SLOs take effect. The precondition can be specified in the *QualifyingCondition* associated with each SLO.

Since the semantics of QoS parameters are not defined precisely in WSAG, we define two types of metrics in WIoT-SLA: measurement directives and composite metrics. The measurement directive is derived from WSLA specification [16], and is directly retrieved from managed resources (e.g., a request URI exposed by the QoS monitor). The composite metrics are created by aggregating measurement directives or other composite metrics according to a function. For example, availability is a composite metric that is composed by a *measurementDirective* (i.e., service uptime and service execution time) with a function (i.e., the ratio of the service uptime to the service execution time).

SLA Template Structure. SLAT is designed as a blueprint to create a valid SLA and SLA negotiation offer, which shares the same structure as the final SLA except for some additional segments. In WIoT-SLA, these segments are (marked in purple on Fig. 3): *CreationConstraint* (optional), *Temporality* (mandatory), *negotiationInformation* (optional) and *Negotiable* indicator (optional) for configuration items or SP variables. The items specified in *CreationConstraint* must be presented in a valid initial negotiation offer and the final SLA with the values satisfying the constraints. We divide constraints into three types: *Range*, *Enumeration* and *Function*. The *Range* type specifies the minimum and maximum value, the *Enumeration* type lists all the possible values, and the *Function* type specifies the value in the form of a function. We define constraints with two attributes: *item* and *targetLocation*, which specifies the name of a term and where to put the constraint respectively. The *targetLocation* can be expressed using a querying languages such as JSONPath[2]. The *Temporality* is defined to indicate the validity date of an SLAT, which is composed of creation timestamp and expiry date. Since the IoT is a large-scale distributed environment

---

[1] WSAG guarantee state model represents a fulfillment state for each GT of an SLA.

[2] https://goessner.net/articles/JsonPath/index.html#e2 - Accessed 15 Jan 2019.

and providers' offerings may change as time passes, the creation timestamp is used to synchronize the latest version of SLAT within the system. The expiry date is used to allow IoT middlewares periodically check the availability of registered SLATs and remove the expired ones to avoid unnecessary interactions during the negotiation stage. The *negotiationInformation* specifies the negotiation interface (i.e., a restful negotiation service EPR or an instant message address) and the negotiation protocol (e.g., CNP or WSAG-Negotiation) if the service is negotiable. If an SLAT does not specify this segment, the service is non-negotiable, and users have to accept all the default values specified in the SLAT. The *Negotiable* indicator is defined to specify the negotiable terms whose values can be changed through negotiation, which means the value in the final SLA can be different from the default value specified in the SLAT. If the indicator is omitted, this means the term is non-negotiable, and it must hold the default value presented in the SLAT.

4.2 Negotiation Offer Ontology

WSAG-Negotiation formalizes negotiation information as *negotiation offers* [26], which are generated based on an SLAT. Generally, the ontology of a negotiation offer (Fig. 6) has four sections: negotiation context (e.g., identifier, party, etc.), offer context, negotiable terms, and negotiation constraints. A negotiation constraint specifies the constraints on negotiable terms when creating a valid counteroffer, which has a similar format to a creation constraint, except that an additional constraint type *FixedValues* is added to indicate the value can not be changed in subsequent offers or the final SLA. The offer state model specified in an offer context controls the interactions between negotiation parties and indicates the rules for taking action after receiving a new offer. For offers in the "rejected" state, to reduce ambiguity and avoid futile interactions, the offer context is extended with domain-specific information to indicate why the offer is rejected. The set of predefined rejected reasons are: { *UnsupportedTerm*, *SLOConflict*, *Timeout*, *InvalidOffer*, *UnderPayment*}. Considering the negotiation offer specified by WSAG-Negotiation might be too heavyweight during the negotiation process, we regulate that the SLAT must be referred in each negotiation offer, and only the terms that specified in *CreationConstraints* or have *Negotiable* indicators will be presented in negotiation offers. Other terms are omitted but regarded as holding the same values presented in the SLAT. Any inconsistency will cause a failure when validating the negotiation offer or creating the final agreement.

5 SLA Template Match-Making

As we described in Sect. 3, SLA negotiation is the first and necessary step to create an SLA before the actual service delivery. Considering the scale of IoT services and possible long latency during a bilateral negotiation process, a template match-making process can reduce the negotiation time by ranking the

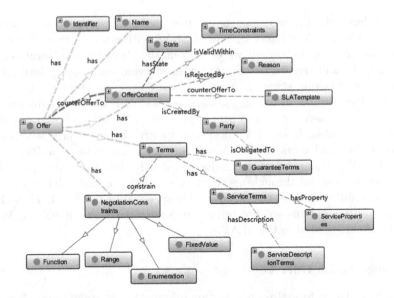

Fig. 6. Ontology of negotiation offer

candidate services based on the similarity between requests and services. Gateways associate an incoming request with registered SLATs that are closest to the requirements, and select the most optimized SLAT to create a negotiation offer. A request is defined as $R = \langle I, O, T, L, F, Q, C^* \rangle$, consisting of inputs, outputs, time, location, functional features (e.g., sample interval), QoS properties, and possibly, the constraints (e.g., the expected price range). We assume providers formalize SLATs by following the WIoT-SLA structure, and the service discovery engine uses a goal-driven backward planning algorithm to discover candidate services based on the semantic relations of service parameters [3]. The matchmaking process is composed of two steps: (i) The candidate SLATs are filtered based on time and spatial features. (ii) The correspondence between the request and each candidate SLAT is measured by the similarity of the request and the SLAT, which is the weighted sum of semantic similarities between the requested terms and the offered terms.

To calculate the semantic similarity of requested terms and services terms, we use an auxiliary source *WordNet* to compute the *WUP* relatedness [11]. A score value greater than 0.75 is regarded as a valid matching. The weight of each valid matching is calculated based on the data type, default value and creation constraints presented in the SLAT. If the feature is negotiable without any creation constraints, the weight w is set to 1. If the feature is negotiable and the value is restricted in the constraints, the weight of a string type is measured by the minimum *Levenshtein distance* [10], and the weight of a numeric type is calculated by Eq. 1 for lower-is-better features (e.g., price or sample interval from a consumer's perspective), and by Eq. 2 for higher-is-better features (e.g., availability or reliability from a consumer's perspective).

$$w = \begin{cases} 1, & \text{if } S_{max} \leq R_{min} \\ \frac{|R \cap S|}{|R|}, & \text{otherwise.} \end{cases} \tag{1}$$

$$w = \begin{cases} 1, & \text{if } S_{min} \geq R_{max} \\ \frac{|R \cap S|}{|R|}, & \text{otherwise.} \end{cases} \tag{2}$$

where S_{max}, S_{min}, R_{max}, R_{max} are the maximum and minimum values of the offered feature and the requested feature respectively. $R \cap S$ is the intersection between the request values and the offered values.

6   Evaluation

A user requests a hazardous gas detection service with functional requirements including minimum sample interval, maximum data deviation, access credential and data reporting protocol, and the QoS requirements including price, availability, reliability and latency. Based on examples proposed in IoT literature [4], we established a SLAT prototype of a gas detection service, and created three datasets based on the prototype. In the first dataset (i.e., test case 1), only 20% services match the request, while in the second dataset (i.e., test case 2), the percentage is increased to 90% (i.e., 10% conflict). For the services that violate the request, 50% of them conflict with the spatial requirements and the rest conflict with the functional or QoS requirements. In the third dataset (i.e., test case 3), 60% services match the request and 60% of them present the same service properties using different words (i.e., using robustness to represent reliability), 40% of them adopt different names as well as data types. In each dataset, 30, 60 and 100 JSON-formatted SLATs are created according to the structure of WIoT-SLA. Theses SLATs are different in terms of configuration items (i.e., different names, synonymous names, different range of values, different data types), SP variables, SLOs and constraints.

The WIoT-SLA match-making algorithm is implemented in Java under Eclipse Mars2 IDE, and the third-party library WS4J[3] is integrated to check words' semantic relatedness. The executable jar file is deployed on three devices: a Dell-OptiPlex-990 desktop (Intel Core i7-2600 CPU, 4 GB DDR3 1333 MHz RAM, Windows 10 OS), a 13-inch MacBook-Pro laptop (Intel Core i5 CPU, 8 GB DDR3 1333 MHz RAM, macOS High Sierra) and a Raspberry Pi-3 (4xCortex-A7 CPU, 1 GB RAM, 16 GB SD card, Raspbian OS). Figure 7 shows the average processing time (APT) on each device as the scale of candidate services increases, and the APT under the first two different test cases respectively. The service scale has a negative impact on the performance of our SLA match-making algorithm (7(a)), but the negative impact can be slightly reduced by adopting location-based filtering (7(b)). From the result, the responsiveness of WIoT-SLA

---

[3] https://code.google.com/archive/p/ws4j/ - Accessed 22 Jan 2019.

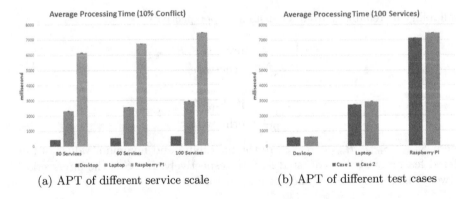

(a) APT of different service scale   (b) APT of different test cases

Fig. 7. Average processing time

match-making is highly dependent on gateways' computational capabilities. For instance, the APT on Dell-OptiPlex-990 (approximately 622 ms) is about 12 times of that on Raspberry Pi-3 (approximately 7438 ms). If we assume gateways are the resource-rich edge devices that can manage hundreds of services that deployed in the local area, such as a desktop or a personal workstation, the latency is acceptable. Otherwise, a more light-weight SLA match-making algorithm is needed for resource-constrained devices selecting the services that have a bigger chance to satisfy all the requirements through SLA negotiation. We further compute the average precision, recall and accuracy in template march-making for test case 3, and compare the result with path-length based similarity (PATH) and Lin similarity (LIN) [11]. Figure 8 presents the result under different thresholds. Among these three approaches, WUP shows a better and more stable performance in a wider range, that's why we select the WUP similarity and set the threshold to 0.75. Although there are services incorrectly matched to the request, considering the high recall, this problem can be solved by ranking the candidate services based on their similarity value and selecting the Top-K solutions as the final candidate services.

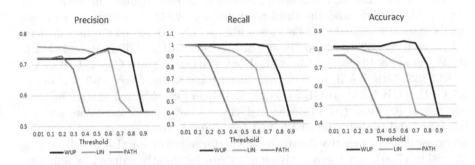

Fig. 8. Precision, recall and accuracy of test case 3

7   Conclusion

This paper proposed an SLA ontology for IoT services that covers the IoT's layered architecture and its domain-specific properties. To achieve semantic interoperability and enable automatic SLA management in the IoT environment, we formalized the SLA schema by extending the commonly used web service SLA specification: WS-Agreement. This schema can be extended by domain-specific experts to construct SLAs for different applications. According to the ontology, we designed a match-making algorithm to select the candidate services which are more likely to provide the service as requested before SLA negotiation. As future work, we aim to develop an SLA reputation system that can audit the SLA's fulfillment based on negotiation and monitoring result, and provide a more lightweight service match-making mechanism resource-constrained IoT gateways.

References

1. Andrieux, A., et al.: Web services agreement specification (WS-agreement). In: Open Grid Forum, vol. 128, p. 216 (2007)
2. Bermudez-Edo, M., Elsaleh, T., Barnaghi, P., Taylor, K.: IoT-Lite: a lightweight semantic model for the Internet of Things. In: 2016 International IEEE Conferences on Ubiquitous Intelligence & Computing, Advanced and Trusted Computing, Scalable Computing and Communications, Cloud and Big Data Computing, Internet of People, and Smart World Congress (UIC/ATC/ScalCom/CBDCom/IoP/SmartWorld), pp. 90–97. IEEE (2016)
3. Cabrera, C., Palade, A., White, G., Clarke, S.: Services in IoT: a service planning model based on consumer feedback. In: Pahl, C., Vukovic, M., Yin, J., Yu, Q. (eds.) ICSOC 2018. LNCS, vol. 11236, pp. 304–313. Springer, Cham (2018). https://doi.org/10.1007/978-3-030-03596-9_21
4. Cabrera, C., White, G., Palade, A., Clarke, S.: The right service at the right place: a service model for smart cities. In: 2018 IEEE International Conference on Pervasive Computing and Communications (PerCom), pp. 1–10. IEEE (2018)
5. Calbimonte, J.P., Riahi, M., Kefalakis, N., Soldatos, J., Zaslavsky, A.: Utility metrics specifications. openiot deliverable d422. Technical report (2014)
6. Chen, D., Varshney, P.K.: QoS support in wireless sensor networks: a survey. In: International Conference on Wireless Networks, vol. 233, pp. 1–7 (2004)
7. Compton, M., et al.: The SSN ontology of the W3C semantic sensor network incubator group. Web Semant.: Sci. Serv. Agents World Wide Web 17, 25–32 (2012). https://doi.org/10.1016/j.websem.2012.05.003. http://www.sciencedirect.com/science/article/pii/S1570826812000571
8. Duan, R., Chen, X., Xing, T.: A QoS architecture for IoT. In: 2011 International Conference on and 4th International Conference on Cyber, Physical and Social Computing Internet of Things (iThings/CPSCom), pp. 717–720. IEEE (2011)
9. Gaillard, G., Barthel, D., Theoleyre, F., Valois, F.: SLA Specification for IoT Operation-The WSN-SLA Framework. Ph.D. thesis, INRIA (2014)
10. Gusfield, D.: Algorithms on Strings, Trees and Sequences: Computer Science and Computational Biology. Cambridge University Press, Cambridge (1997)
11. Jurafsky, D., Martin, J.H.: Speech and Language Processing, vol. 3. Pearson, London (2014)

12. Kazmi, A., Serrano, M., Lenis, A., Soldatos, J.: A QoS-aware integrated management of IoT deployments in smart cities. In: 2017 IEEE 10th Conference on Service-Oriented Computing and Applications (SOCA), pp. 141–146. IEEE (2017)

13. Kearney, K.T., Torelli, F., Kotsokalis, C.: SLA*: an abstract syntax for service level agreements. In: 2010 11th IEEE/ACM International Conference on Grid Computing (GRID), pp. 217–224. IEEE (2010)

14. Kouki, Y., De Oliveira, F.A., Dupont, S., Ledoux, T.: A language support for cloud elasticity management. In: 2014 14th IEEE/ACM International Symposium on Cluster, Cloud and Grid Computing (CCGrid), pp. 206–215. IEEE (2014)

15. Kyriazis, D.: Cloud computing service level agreements-exploitation of research results. European Commission Directorate General Communications Networks Content and Technology Unit, Technical report 5, 29 (2013)

16. Ludwig, H., Keller, A., Dan, A., King, R.P., Franck, R.: Web service level agreement (WSLA) language specification, pp. 815–824. IBM Corporation (2003)

17. Palade, A., Cabrera, C., Li, F., White, G., Razzaque, M., Clarke, S.: Middleware for Internet of Things: an evaluation in a small-scale IoT environment. J. Reliable Intell. Environ. **4**, 1–21 (2018)

18. Papadopoulos, A.V., Asadollah, S.A., Ashjaei, M., Mubeen, S., Pei-Breivold, H., Behnam, M.: SLAs for industrial IoT: mind the gap. In: 2017 5th International Conference on Future Internet of Things and Cloud Workshops (FiCloudW), pp. 75–78. IEEE (2017)

19. Redl, C., Breskovic, I., Brandic, I., Dustdar, S.: Automatic SLA matching and provider selection in grid and cloud computing markets. In: Proceedings of the 2012 ACM/IEEE 13th International Conference on Grid Computing, pp. 85–94. IEEE Computer Society (2012)

20. Soldatos, J., et al.: OpenIoT: open source Internet-of-Things in the cloud. In: Podnar Žarko, I., Pripužić, K., Serrano, M. (eds.) Interoperability and Open-Source Solutions for the Internet of Things. LNCS, vol. 9001, pp. 13–25. Springer, Cham (2015). https://doi.org/10.1007/978-3-319-16546-2_3

21. Swiatek, P., Rucinski, A.: IoT as a service system for eHealth. In: 2013 IEEE 15th International Conference on e-Health Networking, Applications & Services (Healthcom), pp. 81–84. IEEE (2013)

22. Thoma, M., Meyer, S., Sperner, K., Meissner, S., Braun, T.: On IoT-services: survey, classification and enterprise integration. In: 2012 IEEE International Conference on Green Computing and Communications (GreenCom), pp. 257–260. IEEE (2012)

23. Tönjes, R., et al.: Real time IoT stream processing and large-scale data analytics for smart city applications. In: Poster session, European Conference on Networks and Communications (2014)

24. Uriarte, R.B., Tiezzi, F., Nicola, R.D.: SLAC: a formal service-level-agreement language for cloud computing. In: Proceedings of the 2014 IEEE/ACM 7th International Conference on Utility and Cloud Computing, pp. 419–426. IEEE Computer Society (2014)

25. Villalonga, C., Bauer, M., López Aguilar, F., Huang, V.A., Strohbach, M.: A resource model for the real world internet. In: Lukowicz, P., Kunze, K., Kortuem, G. (eds.) EuroSSC 2010. LNCS, vol. 6446, pp. 163–176. Springer, Heidelberg (2010). https://doi.org/10.1007/978-3-642-16982-3_13

26. Waeldrich, O., et al.: WS-Agreement Negotiation Version 1.0, p. 64 (2011)

27. Zheng, X.: QoS representation, negotiation and assurance in cloud services. Queen's University (Canada) (2014)

IoT for Fault Detection in Thailand

Anurak Choeichum[✉], Yutthana Krutgard, and Wichan Inyoo

Provincial Electricity Authority (PEA),
Phra Nakhon Si Ayutthaya 13000, Thailand
anurak.cho@pea.co.th

Abstract. Fault detection and notification in the distribution lines are very important for the operation of the power system. Due to the high cost of communication technology, largely rural area, and so many points of sensor installation, there are limited and difficult to monitoring and data sending. In this paper, we proposed concept using wireless sensor networks that could sense the faulty event in the distribution line, display to the web application as well as send an alarm notification to area distribution dispatching center and service crew, by LoRa network that a low cost, low power, and long-range communication via IoT.

Keywords: Fault detection · Distribution lines · Monitoring · Wireless sensor

1 Introduction

1.1 A Subsection Sample

Fault location and notification are one of the most challenges Provincial Electricity Authority (PEA) must develop, and in particular fault detection in a power distribution system that long line and so many locations. Power outage event after the drop out fuse device in the distribution line is a very necessary problem because in the distribution line fault often occur many times and a long time to fault section finding, these things making the power system unreliable.

This paper employs the current signal to locate the fault sector based on the wireless sensor network (WSN) and send the information [1–4] to monitoring centers or service team with newly implemented LoRa technology for massive and widespread installation.

This implementation used many devices, such as hall-effect current sensor, microcontroller, wireless networks, LoRa networks, IoT module and GSM module, and created the web server and web application for online fault monitoring. When the fault occur in distribution line this system will detect the signal with WSN client node, send the data to LoRa base station with WSN master node, send the data to GSM base station with LoRa base station, and displays the power measurements, status, and event on web browser screen [5, 6].

The objective of this paper is to provide with a new way to detect, send and monitor the fault signal and show the exact section of occurred fault immediately [7].

© Springer Nature Switzerland AG 2019
V. Issarny et al. (Eds.): ICIOT 2019, LNCS 11519, pp. 73–84, 2019.
https://doi.org/10.1007/978-3-030-23357-0_6

2 Sensor and Communication Technologies

The devices are used in this system consists of sensors and various wireless networks. For example the hall-effect current sensor, the wireless sensor networks, the LoRa module, the GSM module, the microcontroller, the AC supply, the solar panel, the charge controller, the battery storage, and the data logger, etc. Each device has different functions and features but we describe the detail of the important device only and will be briefly explained in the following paragraphs.

2.1 Hall-Effect Current Sensor

The Hall Effect is an ideal sensing technology. The Hall Effect sensor is a magnetic field sensor and very popular. When a current-carrying conductor is placed into a magnetic field, a voltage will be generated perpendicular to both the current and the field. For the proposed system, we used the hall-effect current sensors to measure the current and detect fault currents [7] in distribution line.

2.2 Wireless Sensor Networks

The wireless sensor networks are a system composed of numerous computing and sensing devices distributed within an environment to be monitored. The wireless sensors have been intended for fault detection, location, and notification for this system. The wireless sensor networks are useful in reducing power outage duration in the distribution system, [5–7] especially in circuits with many branches.

2.3 LoRa

A LoRa network is wireless modulation technology with features are low power, low bit-rate and long range. The LoRa network uses unlicensed radio spectrum in the ISM bands to enable low power, wide area communication between remote sensors and gateways connected to the network. This system uses internet of things (IoT) technology to send the data from fault section in distribution line to GSM base station and send to the monitoring center.

3 Overview Designed

In this system, we design a communication for fault monitoring as shown in Fig. 1. The communication consists of three part; client node for detecting the fault current, the master node for record the measurement and event, locate section, and send the data to next step, and the base station for send the information to the monitoring center or the web server [4] (Table 1).

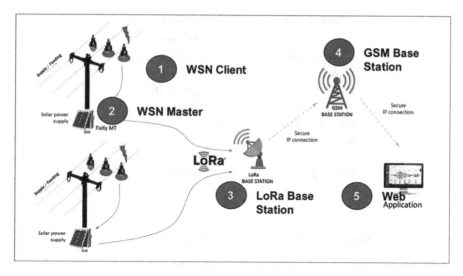

Fig. 1. The overview of this system

3.1 Design of Client Communication

The main of this part is the wireless sensors that used in this system is the Hall Effect current sensor as shown in Fig. 2.

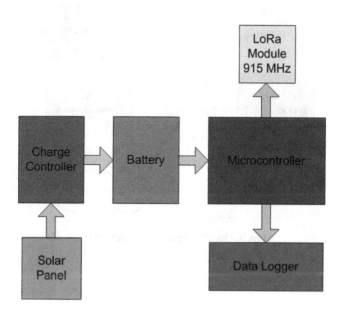

Fig. 2. Block diagram of client node

Table 1. The Equipment used in client node

Type	Operating
ATmega328P	8 MHz/16 MHz
Module 433 Wireless	3.3/3.35–5 V
Battery (Li-ion)	2700 mAh
3D Filament	ABS (g)
Solar Module (Polycrystalline)	80 mA (3 V)
Step-up Module	0.9–5 V
Light	LED
Rubber Seal	Waterproof
Support	Nut/Spring

3.2   Design of Master and Base Station Communication

The master communication used the wireless sensors to get the data from client and send the information to the base station by LoRa technology as shown in Fig. 3. In the base station will forward the information to GSM base station with IoT module via LoRa network for transfer information to the internet as shown in Fig. 4 (Tables 2 and 3).

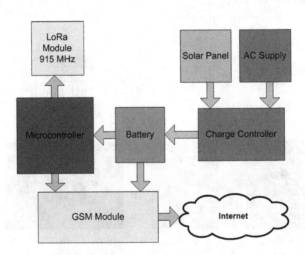

Fig. 3. Block diagram of master node

Table 2. The Equipment used in master node

Type	Operating
ESP-8266EX	80 MHz/160 MHz
Battery (Li-ion)	6 Ah
3D Filament	ABS (g)
Solar Module (Polycrystalline)	80 mA (3 V)
Solar Charge Controller	DC 12 V 10 A
LoRa Module	915 MHz
WiFi Module	5 V 4G LTE
Web Application	Online

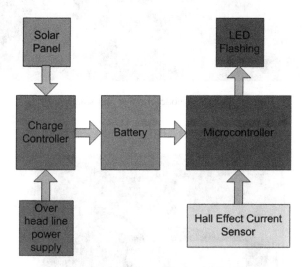

Fig. 4. Block diagram of LoRa base station

Table 3. The equipment used in LoRa base station

Type	Operating
ATmega328P	8 MHz/16 MHz
Module 433 Wireless	3.3/3.35–5 V
Battery (Li-ion)	6 V 6 Ah
3D Filament	ABS (g)
Solar Module (Polycrystalline)	22.2 V 10 W
Solar Charge Controller	DC 12 V 10 A
LoRa Module	915 MHz

4 Implementation

This system used in real in PEA central 1 region 3 in Phra Nakhon Si Ayutthaya Province, Thailand, the device each part as shown in Figs. 5, 6 and 7.

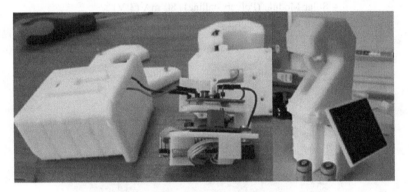

Fig. 5. The client node in cover and solar panel

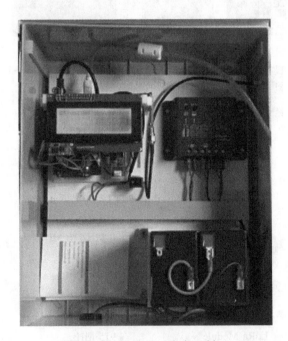

Fig. 6. The master node in cabinet

Fig. 7. The LoRa base station

Fig. 8. The disconnect stick for installation

This client node installation of the system is installed on a high-voltage cable with the use of a disconnect stick as shown in Fig. 8, and in the Fig. 9 shows the client node on high-voltage cable after installation.

Fig. 9. The client node on high-voltage cable after installation

Fig. 10. The master node with solar panel on high-voltage

Fig. 11. The overview of actual sensor installation

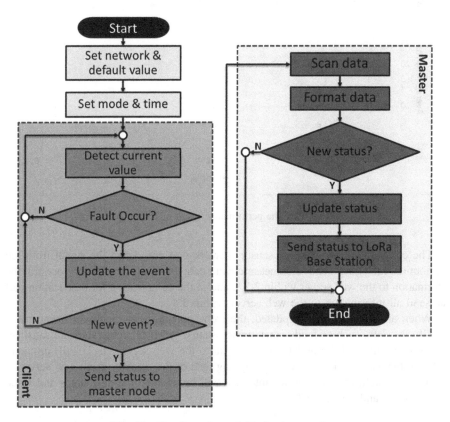

Fig. 12. The flow chart of this implementation

The contribution addressed a real smart grid application, where autonomous sensors monitor current. In the Fig. 10, you can see that this system is designed to be independently powered from solar panels. This work has real practical relevance as shown in Fig. 11. The statements made are well proven by long term trials (Fig. 12).

5   Experimental Results

The test was conducted by applying a user request rate of thousand per minute. A linearly increasing rate of 40/s was applied to test the system performance. This performance guarantee of the server is needed. The result is shown in Fig. 13. The response time is the main performance parameter that the end user can experience directly for the available services. The average response time obtained in this test was 35.94 ms.

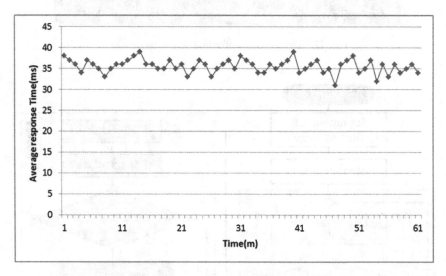

Fig. 13. The performance result of testing

The computation for wireless sensor network part can detect the signal from the distribution line, and send the measurement data to master node for forward the information to the web server within 2.7 s, and in the computation for base station part can send all information to the web server within 3.4 s.

When an event has been updated, the web application at monitoring center will identify the data, such as fault status, device status, etc. If all constraints are satisfied, this system will send the updated digital data to the web server via TCP/IP protocol, and then the web service will check mapping data of the database from web server, if the data is match, the web service interface will be updated the new status and value automatically and immediately.

The web application will repeat this loop until all the data has been changed. For this reason, user can access the web application system for monitoring with web browser as shown in Fig. 14.

The computation for wireless sensor network part can detect the signal from the distribution line, and send the measurement data to master node for forward the information to the web server within 2.7 s, and in the computation for base station part can send all information to the web server within 3.4 s.

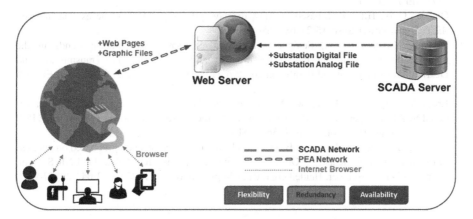

Fig. 14. The web application diagram of this system

6   Conclusion

This proposed system relies on an advantage of the wireless sensor network and the LoRa technology that low cost, low power, and long-range via internet of things for solving fault location in distribution line problem which so many points and far away from the monitoring center.

In this paper, we designed a wireless sensor network and LoRa technology for the online fault monitoring system. This concept successfully locates the fault which occurs in the distribution line and can send the data to the monitoring center or web server which far away.

According to almost one year trial period, this online fault monitoring system is implemented practically, and accurately. This implementation will help service crew or operator to identify the fault section or find the exact fault location. It can be used to monitor the distribution line form anywhere at any time through internet connection, and it can reduce the duration of distribution power outage, increase stability, and enhanced organization standards.

References

1. Genge, B., Beres, A., Haller, P.: A survey on cloud-based software platforms to implement secure smart grids. In: 2014 49th International Universities Power Engineering Conference (UPEC), 2–5 September 2014
2. Leou, R.C., Chang, Y.C., Teng, J.H.: A web-based power quality monitoring system. In: 2001 Power Engineering Society Summer Meeting, vol. 3, pp. 1504–1508. IEEE (2001)
3. Qiu, B., Chen, L., Centeno, V., Dong, X., Liu, Y.: Internet based frequency monitoring network (FNET). In: 2001 Power Engineering Society Winter Meeting, vol. 3, pp. 1166–1171. IEEE (2001)
4. Qiu, B., Gooi, H.B.: Web-based SCADA display systems (WSDS) for access via Internet. IEEE Trans. Power Syst. 15(2), 681–686 (2000)
5. Ishihara, Y., Shirota, Y., Sekiguchi, K., Sato, S., Sawai, K.: Recent trends in the implementation of Intranet based measurement and monitoring. In: Transmission and Distribution Conference and Exhibition 2002: Asia Pacific, vol. 3, pp. 2261–2266. IEEE/PES (2002)
6. Ebata, Y., Hayashi, H., Hasegawa, Y., Komatsu, S., Suzuki, K.: Development of the Intranet-based SCADA (supervisory control and data acquisition system) for power system, IEEE PES Winter meeting 2000, vol. 3, pp. 1656–1661 (2000)
7. Zhang, T.-B., Zhou, Y.-L., Chen, B.-D.: Fault location scheme of smart grid based on wireless sensor networks. In: Sénac, P., Ott, M., Seneviratne, A. (eds.) ICWCA 2011. LNICST, vol. 72, pp. 107–115. Springer, Heidelberg (2012). https://doi.org/10.1007/978-3-642-29157-9_10

IoT-Based Monitoring and Control Systems for Window Energy Management: Design and Implementation

Yoon G. Kim[1]([⊠]), Shenghui Chen[1], Timothy Dykhuis[1],
John Slagter[2], and Matthew Nauta[2]

[1] Calvin College, Grand Rapids, MI 49546, USA
ygk2@calvin.edu
[2] Mackinac Technology Company, Kentwood, MI 49512, USA

Abstract. This paper presents the design and implementation of an IoT-based system for window energy management. The system computes thermal transmittances of window units and solar heat gain coefficients through window units from measured sensor readings. It is critical to have energy efficient windows in homes and offices so as to conserve energy. In order to test the performance of the window units in realistic environments we created a system which can be used outdoors at any time. It is convenient for a user to control the system and access the measured data from a remote or even mobile site. The goal of this work was to design and implement a system that measures sensor data, transmits the data over a wireless communication link, distributes the data through the Internet, and stores the data in a database for analysis at any time and anywhere. The IoT is a computer network, in which anyone and anything can connect together anytime and anywhere [1]. It is realizable through sensing and communication technologies [2]. The IoT approach was adopted to achieve our goal due to the availability of sensing technology, wireless communication technologies, and standard computer networking protocols. We designed and implemented a system for calculating the thermal energy related parameters of the window units. The measured data from sensors were transmitted to a cloud server over cellular networks and the Internet. The data in the server can be accessed, stored, and displayed remotely. As long as electricity and cellular phone networks are available, the system can connect sensors to users. Extensive testing was conducted to verify the operation of the system. The testing and measurement results show that the system successfully performs the necessary operations to achieve the goal.

Keywords: Internet of Things (IoT) application ·
Window energy management · U-factor · Solar heat gain

1 Introduction

The Internet of Things (IoT) is an emerging technology that draws increasing interest in industry and also in the research community [2, 3]. The term IoT was first coined in 1999 [4] and reported by the International Telecommunication Union (ITU) in 2005

© Springer Nature Switzerland AG 2019
V. Issarny et al. (Eds.): ICIOT 2019, LNCS 11519, pp. 85–98, 2019.
https://doi.org/10.1007/978-3-030-23357-0_7

[1]. The IoT concept in the report embraces a vision of ubiquitous networks, in which anyone and anything (RFID tag or computing device with sensors, etc.) can connect together anytime (24/7) and anywhere (indoor, outdoor, or on the move). One of the definitions of IoT considers IoT as a network of interconnected objects based on standard communication protocols [5]. The terms "objects", "things", and "devices" are used interchangeably in the IoT articles [6]. The object can have a sensor, multiple sensors of the same type, or multiple sensors of different types. When the objects are interconnected, a sensor network is formed. In terms of sensor networks, the IoT network can be described as sensor networks connected over the Internet [6]. The IoT has industrial applications in healthcare service, the food supply chain, transportation, logistics, environmental monitoring [3], and modern manufacturing [7]. A study [8] classifies IoT solutions based on the IoT application domain. The IoT concept can be realizable through integrating enabling technologies: identification with RFID tags, sensor networks, and current communication technologies [2].

Due to the availability of sensors, current communication technologies, and standard computer networking protocols, the IoT approach was adopted to achieve our goal in this project. The main goal of the project was to design and implement a system which can measure sensor data, transmit the data over a wireless communication link, and distribute the data using standard computer networking protocols anytime and anywhere. In this case, the system reports thermal energy related parameters on window units.

It is reported that there are significant energy losses through building windows [9]. Insulated windows are being developed to conserve energy. U-factor or U-value is a measure of thermal transmittance. It represents "how much energy will be lost from a building through its windows" [10]. The lower the U-factor, the better the window insulates. A standard test method was developed to measure the U-factor using hot box methods [11]. Through the hot box method, the U-factor can be calculated as [11]

$$U_s = Q_s/[A_s \times (t_h - t_c)] \tag{1}$$

where U_s is thermal transmittance of test specimen (e.g., window), A_s is the projected area of a surrounding panel, Q_s is the time rate of heat flow through the test specimen, t_h is the temperature of the hot side of the hot box, and t_c is the cold side temperature of the hot box. The quantity Q_s is determined by

$$Q_s = Q_{heater} - Q_{wall} - Q_{box} \tag{2}$$

where Q_{heater} is the electrical power put into the heater, Q_{wall} is the heat loss through the walls surrounding the window, and Q_{box} is the heat loss through the hot box. The overall thermal resistance of a test specimen is called R_s [11] and is commonly used in the building industry and defined as

$$R_s = 1/U_s \tag{3}$$

Recently, a cost-effective retrofit window insulation system was developed using highly transparent window films to reduce heat losses [12]. The window units were evaluated by measuring the R-value (R_s) using the hot box methods. This paper explains how we extend the previous work in order to test the window units in more realistic environments emulating a building setting where the heat source is sunlight. We developed a unique type of IoT-based system to be operated with and installed in the Window Energy Management System (WEMS^{TM}) [13] Test Box, which can be used outdoors anytime. The system is designed to measure the solar heat gain coefficient (SHGC) [14], which represents the radiant heat transmitted to an enclosure through a window. The R-values are also measured in situ using the center of glazing method [15]. The system can measure the SHGC and R-values of window units remotely by monitoring and controlling the associated modules of the system using wireless communications and computer networking protocols. The system can run 24/7 as long as it can access electricity and cellular phone networks. It is an IoT-based system as it includes sensors, embedded systems, actuators, wireless communications, and Internet cloud servers, which are the core components of IoT technology.

The rest of the paper is organized into sections as follows: In Sect. 2, the design and implementation of the proposed system are discussed. We illustrate the block diagram of the proposed system and present photos of implemented control systems for window energy management. Then, we explain the functionalities of each block and the relationship between the blocks in the diagram. Section 3 explains the embedded controller software. We focus on presenting the functionality of the application programs we developed. In Sect. 4, testing and measurement results are presented. Concluding remarks are presented in Sect. 5.

2 Design and Implementation of the Proposed System

This project required measurement of physical quantities, such as temperatures and pressures, from many sensors. The measurement data needed to be collected, then stored, and processed to evaluate the system under test.

Figure 1 shows the block diagram of the system implemented. The cellular 4G LTE router [16] connects the test box to a Message Queuing Telemetry Transport (MQTT) [17] server and a cloud database, MongoDB Atlas [18] server, through the Internet. The Command Center connects these servers remotely to access its data transmitted from the test box. The main controller of the system is the embedded system, Raspberry Pi 3 B + [19], which controls the cellular router, the Wi-Fi router, the fan control unit, and the data acquisition (DAQ) unit as shown in the figure. The detailed descriptions of the software of the embedded system are presented in Sect. 3.

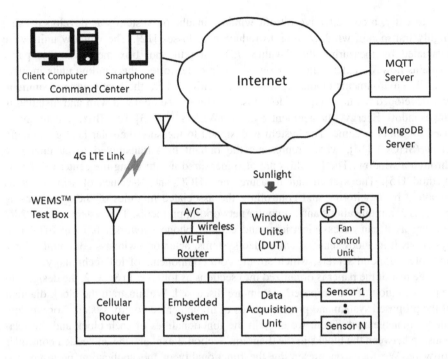

Fig. 1. Block diagram of proposed IoT-based system

The Wi-Fi router is used to connect the cellular router to the air conditioning unit, which has Wi-Fi connectivity. There are two fans inside the test box, adjusted by the fan control unit. The unit reads the current temperature or process value (PV) in the chamber where the windows units are installed and compares the setpoint value (SV). The unit adjusts the speed of the fan to minimize the difference between PV and SV in a closed-loop fashion. The SV can be configured via relay boards connected to the fan control unit by a user at the Command Center, remotely through the Internet. The DAQ unit has total of 64 single-ended input channels or 32 differential input channels [20]. Twenty four (24) thermocouples are used to measure the temperature in the chamber and on the window surfaces. Two pressure sensors [21] are used to measure the air mass flow rate at the inlet and outlet orifices. The flow rate is utilized to calculate heat transfer rate in the test box chamber interior of the window units, which allows us to compute the heat flow rate due to solar radiant heat transmitted into the chamber. The solar heat rate is utilized to determine the solar heat gain coefficient (SHGC).

All sensors are attached to the DAQ, which converts analog signals from sensors to digital data with 24-bit resolution every 1 min since the temperature being measured varies relatively slowly. The appearance of the implemented WEMS^{TM} Test Box is shown in Fig. 2. The overall size of the system is 8 (W) × 8 (L) × 8 (H) feet excluding the roof and its air vent.

Fig. 2. Appearance of the test box in Fig. 1

Figure 3 shows the internal view of the test box (A/C, fans, and window units not shown). The DC power supply provides DC 24 V to the cellular router and the DC-to-DC converters, which provide DC 5 V and DC 9 V to low voltage circuits (such as the embedded controller, relay boards, DAQ, sensors, and Wi-Fi router).

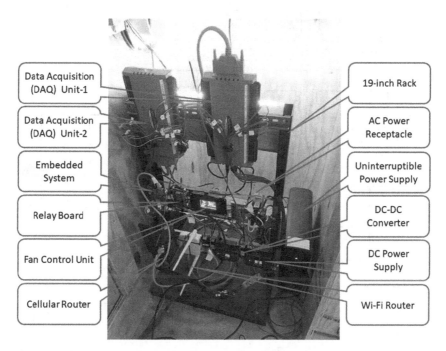

Fig. 3. Implementation of control system for the test box

The detail connection diagram is shown in Fig. 4. The red arrows represent power connections and the blue arrows represent signal connections.

The average data rate being sent from the embedded system to the cellular router should be less than the transmission throughput of the router whose memory size is finite. The measured average throughput of the router ranges between 1.3 Mbps and 7.6 Mbps, which was measured in Michigan, USA during the weekdays. The total average data rate [bits per second] can be calculated as follows.

$$
\begin{aligned}
\text{Avg. Data Rate} &= \{\# \text{ of ch} \times (\text{ch numbers} + \text{delimiters} + \text{values})\} \text{samples/min} \\
&= \{32 \times (6 \text{ bytes} + 5 \text{ bytes})\}/60 \sec \\
&= 2,816 \text{ bits}/60 \sec = 46.9 \, [\text{bps}]
\end{aligned}
\tag{4}
$$

As the measured throughput (1.3–7.6 Mbps) of the cellular router is practically much larger than the average data rate above, the wireless transmission through the cellular link is considered to have enough bandwidth for reliable communication. The cellular link was chosen for its large coverage and relative low cost with moderate bandwidth.

The sampled data by the DAQ are temporarily stored in the memory of embedded system and pushed to the MQTT server. We use CloudMQTT [22] for implementing the MQTT server. The data in the server can be accessed by a user remotely at the Command Center.

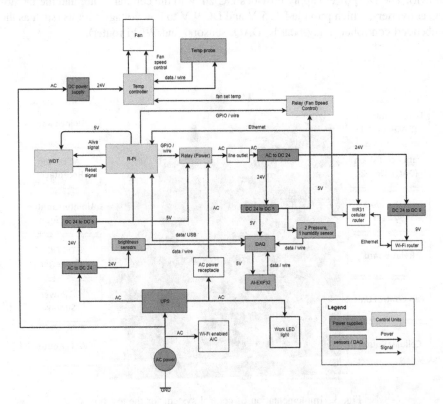

Fig. 4. Connection diagram of the control system for the test box (Color figure online)

When the system is operated remotely, automated maintenance features and user-initiated remote maintenance features are often needed to cope with situations where abnormalities occurs in the test box. The automated maintenance features include (1) a watchdog timer (WDT) and (2) cellular link wake-up. The user-initiated remote maintenance features include remote rebooting and remote power cycling of routers and the DAQ. For example, when the embedded controller is halted, e.g., due to glitches on the DC power, the WDT circuit reboots the controller. This operation uses two signals connected to the embedded controller I/O pins as shown in Fig. 4. The embedded controller sends a signal (Alive) every minute. When this is received, a timer in the WDT circuit is restarted, and there is no action. If the signal (Alive) is not received for over three minutes, a signal (Reset) is sent to the controller for reboot.

The cellular router's connectivity to the Internet is monitored every thirty minutes by an embedded controller program. When the program detects errors on the Internet connection to the MQTT server, it automatically turns the Relay (Power) OFF, waits for five seconds, then back ON. This operation is to run a power cycle on the cellular router, the Wi-Fi router, and the DAQ. A user at the Command Center can also run the power cycle manually by accessing the MQTT server if needed.

3 Embedded Control Software

The embedded controller runs the control software to ensure the operation of the test box. This software includes an operating system (OS) based on Debian [23], a DAQ driver, open-source code, and the application programs we developed. This section presents the functionality of the application programs we developed, which are Watchdog_Pat, Wakeup_Post, Command_Receive, Data_Post, Internet_Check, and Test_Box.

/etc./rc.local file on the embedded systems is executed automatically during the boot process. The file includes Watchdog_Pat, Wakeup_Post, and Command_Receive. The last program is in an infinite loop and run in a separate process from a main program.

crond (cron daemon) is the name of a daemon which runs in the background of the OS and reads a file called crontab (cron table) [24]. It allows shell commands to run periodically. There are three programs listed in the crontab: Watchdog_Pat, Data_Post, and Internet_Check.

Table 1 shows the name of programs and associated period of calls.

Table 1. Application programs and period of call

Application program	Period of call
Watchdog_Pat	1 min
Data_Post	1 min
Internet_Check	30 min

The Watchdog_Pat program is not only called by the crond every minute but also called during the boot process to prevent the watchdog timer from being timed out during the process. The program manipulates the signal on the GPIO pin of the embedded controller to refresh the WDT circuit.

The names of the MQTT topics in this project are 'debug1', 'command1', and 'sunbox1'.

The Wakeup_Post uses a program called mosquitto [25], which is installed on the embedded controller, to publish a message on the 'debug1' topic to the MQTT server. It establishes a connection to the server. The Wakeup_Post publishes a message to show that the embedded controller booted successfully and to provide the controller's current IP address.

The Data_Post program creates a connection between the embedded controller and the MQTT server and then publishes messages on the 'sunbox1' topic. These messages are the readings of sensors attached to the DAQs. To obtain the readings, the Data_Post utilizes the DAQ device driver [26].

The Internet_Check program checks the Internet connection by attempting to connect to the MQTT server. The program uses the return value as a flag to indicate the success of the connection process. If it is not successful, the program initiates the power cycling of two routers to restart the Internet connection. If it is successful, it does nothing. This software is called every 30 min by the crond.

The Command_Receive program allows the embedded controller to receive a remote message from the MQTT server in which a user enters the message under the 'command1' topic on the CloudMQTT server screen as shown in Fig. 6. The program listens to a message published on a specific topic ('command1') and responds to four messages: 'u' for increasing the temperature setpoint value of the fan controller, 'd' for decreasing the value, 'p' for power cycling, and 'r' for restarting the embedded controller only. The program publishes a message on the 'debug1' topic when the connection to CloudMQTT is established successfully and when the embedded controller receives a valid command through the 'command1' topic. The Command_Receive program uses an open-source implementation of MQTT, paho.mqtt [27], to communicate with the MQTT server.

The Test_Box program allows the embedded controller to perform the heat flow rate calculations. This rate is integral to finding the SHGC. The program uploads the processed data to the MongoDB Atlas.

Increasing or decreasing the fan commands 'u' or 'd' are accomplished through the GPIO pins of the embedded controller. The voltages on the pins drive the relay board to close or open the pushbutton on the fan control unit shown in Fig. 3. The power cycle command 'p' is accomplished through the GPIO pins of the embedded controller, too. It runs a power cycle on the cellular router, the Wi-Fi router, and DAQ to restart. The restart command 'r' is accomplished through the restart command in the operating system.

We developed a program named mqtt_pub_sub to run on the Command Center PC. The program subscribes the 'sunbox1' topic so that the server can receive measurement data (messages) from the embedded controller in the test box. The program also publishes the message ('u', 'd', 'p', or 'r') on the 'command1' topic to display the message on the CloudMQTT screen as shown in Fig. 6.

A database is installed on the Command Center PC to have all the measurement readings from the test box stored locally on the PC. The database used for this purpose is MongoDB [27]. When new data is published on the 'sunbox1' topic, the mqtt_pub_sub program reads the data, parses it into corresponding fields, and stores it in the database.

The software list and devices that run the software are shown in Table 2.

Table 2. Devices and software

Device	Software
Embedded controller	Debian OS, DAQ Device Driver, paho.mqtt, mosquitto, Command_Receive, Data_Post, Wakeup_Post, Watchdog_Pat, Internet_Check, Test_Box
Command center PC	mqtt_pub_sub, MongoDB
Cloud server	CloudMQTT, MongoDB Atlas

4 Testing and Results

When the embedded controller gets booted, two messages are published on the 'debug1' topic as shown in the blue box of Fig. 5.

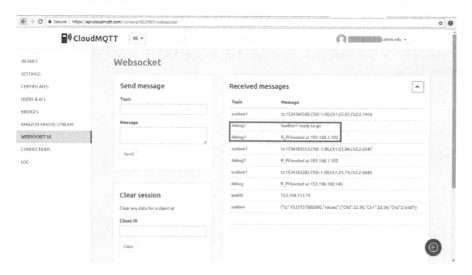

Fig. 5. Messages during boot process (Color figure online)

When a user at the Command Center types in 'command1' in the Topic box and 'u' in the Message box followed by clicking on the Send button, the message is published on the 'command1' topic and delivered to the embedded controller. After the Command_Receive program running on the embedded controller receives any of the four messages listed above, the program acts according to the messages. It also publishes a message under the 'debug1' topic on the server acknowledging the reception of the command. This is shown in the blue box of Fig. 6.

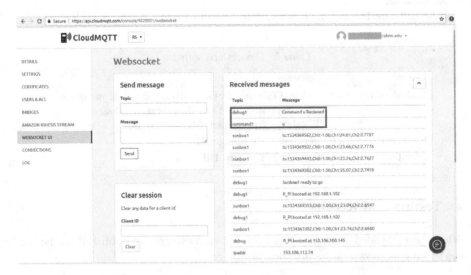

Fig. 6. Topics and messages by Command_Receive (Color figure online)

The Data_Post on the embedded controller publishes measured temperature values as messages on the 'sunbox1' topic, sending to the MQTT server every minute as shown in Fig. 7.

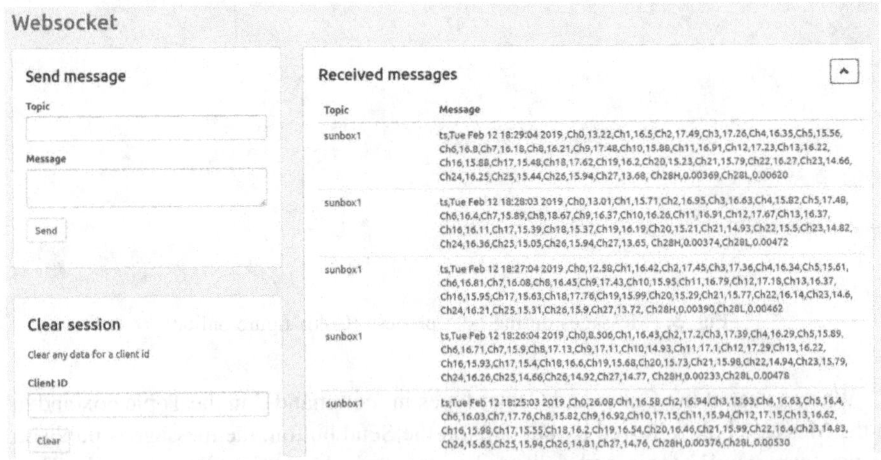

Fig. 7. Measurement data published as messages by Data_Post

The messages in Fig. 7 are in the form of a string. The string has fields that are separated by commas. The first field text "ts" stands for "time stamp". The next field is the time stamp of the message followed including day, time, and year. The field after the time stamp is "Ch0", indicating that the following field is the temperature in Celsius of the thermocouple connected to channel 0 of the DAQ. The same rule applies to the readings from channels 0–13 and channels 16–27. Note that the channels 14 and 15 are reserved for future use. The differential input of Channel 28 is used to measure pressures from two single-ended pressure sensors. The value following the field "Ch28H" is the pressure reading of the sensor attached to the + terminal of the channel 28 of the DAQ. Similarly, "Ch28L" refers to the pressure sensor connected to the terminal of the channel 28.

Once the Test_Box program uploads the processed data to MongoDB Atlas, charts can easily be made and customized within a MongoDB dashboard. Variables from the database are dragged to applicable fields depending on chart type for the X-axis and Y-axis values. Charts automatically update with new data, though filters may be used to select specific date ranges. Labels, colors, and other chart elements may also be customized within the chart-creation window. Figures 8, 9, and 10 illustrate the charts of time-indexed interior chamber temperature, air mass flow rate, and heat flow rate of the test box, respectively.

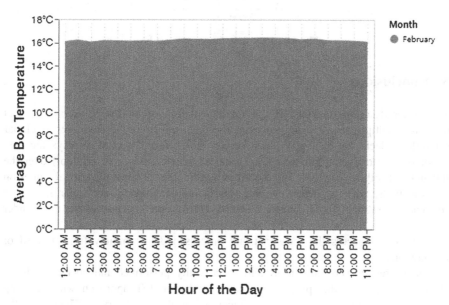

Fig. 8. Interior chamber temperature of the test box

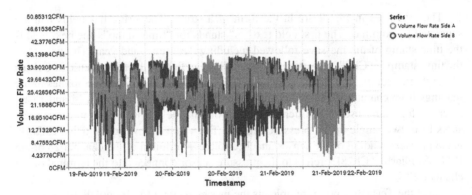

Fig. 9. Air mass flow rate of the test box

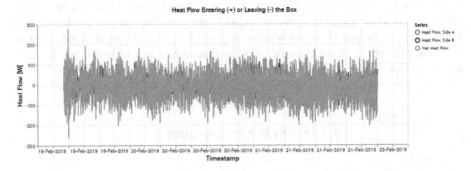

Fig. 10. Heat flow rate of the test box

5 Conclusions

This paper describes the design and implementation of an IoT-based system that measures multiple sensor data, processes the data, transmits the data over a cellular network, collects the data in a cloud server, stores the data, and displays the data remotely. It can operate anytime (24/7) and anywhere (indoor or outdoor) over the Internet and cellular network. The described system can calculate the critical values on window units, such as heat flow rate, thermal transmittance, and solar heat gain coefficient using the stored data for assessing thermal performance of the units under test.

A user can access the measured and processed data remotely from a fixed or moving site.

As the results showed, the system successfully performed the operations listed above. The goal of this project was achieved by an IoT approach with enabling technologies. The processed data were transferred to the cloud servers. The data in the database server were accessed and displayed remotely at the Command Center. Due to the automated maintenance features we developed, the system provides reliable operation.

Through the design and implementation of this project, an IoT-based system for window energy management was realized in an industrial application.

Acknowledgment. The authors thank Dr. Rich DeJong, Dr. Randy Brouwer, and Mr. Leonard Pearlman for valuable input and discussion. The IoT-based system was designed and implemented at Calvin College with funds provided by the 2018 Engineering Sustainability Research Fund. The construction of the WEMS^{TM} Test Box and installation of the IoT-based system were conducted at Mackinac Technology Company and funded under PE 0603734A, Project T15 Military Engineering Technology Demonstration (Congressional Add), Task 07 under Contract W9132T-19-C-0001, managed by the US Army Engineer Research and Development Center, with permission granted by the Director, Construction Engineering Research Laboratory to publish this information.

References

1. International Telecommunication Union: ITU Internet Report 2005: The Internet of Things, https://www.itu.int/net/wsis/tunis/newsroom/stats/The-Internet-of-Things-2005.pdf. Accessed 07 Jan 2019

2. Atzori, L., Iera, A., Morabito, G.: The Internet of Things: a survey. Comput. Netw. **54**(15), 2787–2805 (2010)

3. Xu, L.D., et al.: Internet of Things in industries: a survey. IEEE Trans. Industr. Inf. **10**(4), 2233–2243 (2014)

4. Ashton, K.: That 'Internet of things' Thing. http://www.rfidjournal.com/articles/view?4986. Accessed 07 Jan 2019

5. European Commission: Internet of Things in 2020. https://docbox.etsi.org/erm/Open/CERP-IoT20090518/Internet-of-Things_in_2020_EC-EPoSS_Workshop_Report_2008_v3.pdf. Accessed 07 Jan 2019

6. Perera, C., Zaslavsky, A., Christen, P., Georgakopoulos, D.: Context aware computing for the Internet of Things: a survey. IEEE Commun. Surv. Tutorials **16**(1), 414–454 (2014)

7. Bi, Z., Xu, L.D.: Internet of Things for enterprise systems of modern manufacturing. IEEE Trans. Industr. Inf. **10**(2), 1537–1546 (2014)

8. Perera, C., Liu, C.H., Jayawardena, S.: The emerging Internet of Things marketplace from an industrial perspective: a survey. IEEE Trans. Emerg. Top. Comput. **3**(4), 585–598 (2015)

9. U.S. Department of Energy: Update or Replace Windows. https://www.energy.gov/energysaver/design/windows-doors-and-skylights/update-or-replace-windows. Accessed 07 Jan 2019

10. NFRC: Understanding Window U-Factor. https://www.nfrccommunity.org/blogpost/925129/226115/Understanding-Window-U-Factor. Accessed 07 Jan 2019

11. ASTM: Standard Test Method for Measuring the Steady-State Thermal Transmittance of Fenestration Systems Using Hot Box Methods. https://compass.astm.org/EDIT/html_annot.cgi?C1199+14. Accessed 07 Jan 2019

12. ARPA-E: Single Pane Window Retrofit System. https://arpa-e.energy.gov/?q=slick-sheet-project/single-pane-window-retrofit-system. Accessed 07 Jan 2019

13. Mackinac Technology Company: Mackinac WEMS. https://www.mackinac-technology.com/our-product.html. Accessed 07 Jan 2019

14. U.S. Department of Energy: Energy Performance Ratings for Windows, Doors, and Skylights, https://www.energy.gov/energysaver/design/windows-doors-and-skylights/energy-performance-ratings-windows-doors-and. Accessed 07 Jan 2019

15. NFRC.NFRC 100-2017 [E0A2]: https://www.nfrccommunity.org/store/ViewProduct.aspx?id=1403208. Accessed 07 Jan 2019
16. DIGI. TransPort WR31: https://www.digi.com/products/models/wr31-m52a-de1-tb. Accessed 07 Jan 2019
17. MQTT.org: MQTT. http://mqtt.org/. Accessed 07 Jan 2019
18. MongoDB: MongoDB. https://www.mongodb.com/. Accessed 07 Jan 2019
19. Raspberrypi.org: Raspberry Pi. https://www.raspberrypi.org/. Accessed 07 Jan 2019
20. Measurement Computing: USB-2416 Series. https://www.mccdaq.com/usb-data-acquisition/USB-2416-Series.aspx. Accessed 07 Jan 2019
21. Honeywell: Board Mount Pressure Sensors. https://sensing.honeywell.com/index.php?ci_id=151134. Accessed 07 Jan 2019
22. Cloudmqtt: CloudMQTT. https://www.cloudmqtt.com/. Accessed 07 Jan 2019
23. Debian: Debian OS. https://www.debian.org/. Accessed 07 Jan 2019
24. Opensource: How to use cron in Linux, https://opensource.com/article/17/11/how-use-cron-linux. Accessed 07 Jan 2019
25. Mosquitto.org: Eclipse Mosquitto. https://mosquitto.org/. Accessed 07 Jan 2019
26. Measurement Computing: Third-Party Linux Support. https://www.mccdaq.com/daq-software/Linux-Support.aspx. Accessed 07 Jan 2019
27. Eclipse.org: Eclipse Paho. https://www.eclipse.org/paho/. Accessed 07 Jan 2019

Online Conditions Monitoring of End-Mill Based on Sensor Integrated Smart Holder

Zhaowu Zhan$^{(\boxtimes)}$, Kai Xie, Letian Rong, and Wei Luo

Fuhuake Precision Industry (Shenzhen) Co., Ltd., Foxconn Technology Group,
Shenzhen, China
`zhaowu.zhan@gmail.com`,
`{kai-k.xie,le-tian.rong,wei-w.luo}@fii-foxconn.com`

Abstract. End-mill damage causes the losses of surface smooth and dimensional accuracy for the machined part. In addition, offline monitoring of the end-mill conditions causes downtime and consequently reduce productive efficiency. In order to sense and monitor the conditions of end-mill in real time, an intelligent Internet of Things (IoT) system dedicated to online conditions monitoring of end-mill has been developed in this research work. The designed smart holder highly integrated with tri-axial acceleration sensor, Micro Controller Unit (MCU), wireless radio chip and battery is demonstrated. The system collects high resolution end-milling data during cutting without interfering with the machining process. In order to extract the data sequence containing the information highly related to the conditions of the end-mill, a simple but effective data extraction algorithm based on sinusoidal correlation is proposed. By real-time exploring the extracted data sequence via the developed data mining algorithm on the Computerized Numerical Control (CNC) edge server, the conditions of end-mill can be monitored online and consequently decision can be made in real time.

Keywords: IoT · End-Mill · Sensor · Smart holder · CNC ·
Edge server · Feature extraction · Condition monitoring

1 Introduction

Nowadays, smart manufacturing is a hot topic and attracts great attentions both from academia and industry. The demands for high-speed, high-accuracy, high-efficiency cutting and grinding continue to grow due to the increasing need for quick machining and delivery of workpieces with a variety of complicated shapes. However, downtime caused by the tool failure and possible consequent machine damage is an important economical factor since downtime cost is high. Besides, overuse or underuse of the end-mill will have negative economical impacts. Overuse of the end-mill will cause failure products while underuse of end-mill

This work is supported by Shenzhen Science and Technology Program.

V. Issarny et al. (Eds.): ICIOT 2019, LNCS 11519, pp. 99–113, 2019.
https://doi.org/10.1007/978-3-030-23357-0_8

will make waste of the residual life of that. Additionally, optimization of machining process based on the available full knowledge of end-mill conditions can be fulfilled globally. End-mill online monitoring and prediction are generally considered to be among the most important problems in realizing modern smart manufacturing. Implementation of a reliable end-mill condition online monitoring and prediction system should allow the end-mill state information to be sent to the server in real time. According to online data-mining in the IoT server, suggestion of suitable adaptive and/or corrective action will be given immediately. Therefore, on-line conditions monitoring of end-mill is a meaningful work. However, due to the complexity of the cutting process and high requirement of the hardware, on-line conditions monitoring of end-mill is also a big challenging work.

The papers [1,5] present a method of end-mill conditions monitoring tembased on thermal image with a high speed thermography, in which temperature information is explored. The researchers in [2] developed a *Tool Condition Monitoring* (TCM) system based on wireless triaxial accelerometer, while the accelerometer is mounted on the workpiece which can't guarantee providing high sensitivity of conditions monitoring especially for small-diameter end-mills.

The fact that vibration signal contains useful information related to the condition of the equipment has been demonstrated by [3,4]. By corresponding the extracted features of the vibration signal to the physical characteristics of end-mill, the conditions monitoring of tool wear can be realized.

Tool wear causes the friction between cutting lips and surrounding workpiece material, which consequently leads to the vibration including vibration frequency and magnitude. The variations of vibration magnitude are most likely related to the tool wear process conditions and therefore will indirectly reflect the conditions of end-mill. Historically, the ability to record in-process data about the vibration of end-mill has been limited to data collected from sensors at the locations physically distant from the cutting process. Often, these sensors are mounted on the material workpiece or the machine spindle. Due to the complexity of *Computerized Numerical Control* (CNC) system, the vibration signal transmitted from the tool tips to the location of a traditionally mounted stationary sensor is high noisily interfered. This fact increases the difficulty of extracting end-mill conditions from the sensor data. In order to reduce or even eliminate the effect of transmission noise and extract the real tool tip response characteristics during the cutting process, the sensor device should be mounted as close to the tool tip as possible.

In this paper, we employ the conventional fact that vibration signal containing useful information can be exploited to monitor the conditions of end-mill. Furthermore, a smart holder consisting of and highly integrated with smart sensor and holder, which minimizes the distance between end-mill and sensor and reduces the transmission noise to its minimum, is developed and demonstrated. Additionally, a simple but efficient and practical data extraction method is proposed to mitigate the influence of interference data. Based on the proposed data extraction method, a data-mining algorithm is developed to monitor the conditions of end-mill.

The remainder of this paper is divided into five Sections. The system model including smart device, wireless network and CNC edge server is described in Sect. 2. How to extract exactly the data sequence containing the conditions information of end-mill is given in Sect. 3. Section 4 focuses on digging the data sequence and consequently extracting features which are highly correlated to the conditions of end-mill. The developed system and designed algorithms are system level demonstrated by experiments and experimental results in Sect. 5. Finally, the conclusions and future work are drawn in Sect. 6.

2 System Model

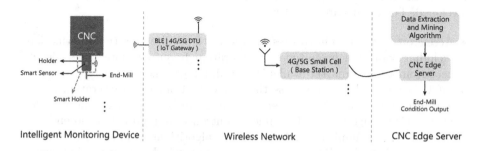

Fig. 1. System architecture of end-mill online conditions monitoring.

System architecture as shown in Fig. 1 includes intelligent monitoring device, wireless network and CNC edge server. The function of intelligent monitoring device is to cut the metal materials while sensing the condition of tool tip and sending it out via wireless radio-on-chip. The function of wireless network is to transmit and gather accelerometer datas. This component includes data collection from the intelligent monitoring device to *Bluetooth Low Energy* (BLE) gateway via BLE wireless technology and data collection from the BLE gateway to the 4G/5G[1] small cell station via 4G/5G wireless technology, and also includes the data transmission from the small cell station to the CNC edge server via ethernet. The main function of the CNC edge server is to store the acquired raw data and support the implementations of data extraction and mining algorithms, and consequently output the decided conditions of the end-mill.

2.1 Intelligent Monitoring Device

The developed intelligent monitoring device includes a spindle, a smart holder and an end-mill. The smart holder is a holder highly integrated with a smart sensor device, which is one of the contributions of this paper and will be elaborated separately in the followings.

---

[1] The fourth/fifth generation of broadband cellular network technology.

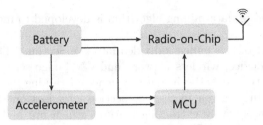

Fig. 2. Diagram of smart sensor device.

Smart Sensor Device. Smart sensor device is one of the key components of intelligent monitoring device. In order to make the sensor work remotely and independently, several highly required function models as shown in Fig. 2 are developed. The details are as follows:

- Accelerometer is used in this research work to acquire vibration information, including vibration magnitude and vibration frequency data. The selected accelerometer is a market-available digital, tri-axial accelerometer.
- MCU is required to preprocess the raw data from the acceleration sensor and format it as an encoded version which can be recognized and decoded by the CNC edge server. This micro controller unit provide a potential of implementing a number of data processing algorithms and models therein. In this research work, ARM Cortex-M3 processor, which is powerful but cheap, is selected as the main CPU. The power consumption of the ARM Cortex-M3 is only 4.5 mW when running at target 50 MHz, and the voltage of power supply of that range from 1.65 V to 3.6 V.
- Radio-on-Chip is used to send the formatted acceleration sensor data over the antenna to the IoT gateway. But in practice, the end-mill is highly spinning with the holder during cutting process. Therefore, the transceiver should be designed to a wireless transceiver. In order to meet the low power consumption demand and support 1.5 Mbps data rate at least, Bluetooth low energy technology, namely IEEE 802.15.1, is selected for data collection from the distributed CNCs to the IoT gateway which is constructed by a BLE master and a 4G/5G *Data Terminal Unit* (DTU). The peak current consumption of the selected BLE is smaller than 15 mA. The voltage of power supply of the selected BLE ranges from 2 V to 3.6 V.
- Battery is required here to supply electrical power via micro *Universal Serial Bus* (USB) to the smart sensor device including MCU, radio-on-chip and accelerometer, which is as shown in Fig. 2. Battery is highly integrated in the holder with smart sensor device. In order to reuse the holder, rechargeable lithium battery is chosen for power supply. The output voltage of the battery is 3 V, which can meet the requirement of device's power supply. Besides, the power consumption of the accelerometer is negligible compared to that of MCU and BLE radio-on-chip. Based on the power consumption of each component of the smart sensor device, the capacity of the chosen battery

should be at least 3000 mAh to guarantee that the intelligent monitoring device can work continuously for seven days without any interruption due to battery recharge.

By fully and efficiently organizing these models, the smart sensor device can be highly integrated into the tool holder without ruining the dynamic balance of the traditional tool holder and work efficiently under very high spinning condition without wire contact.

Smart Holder. Smart holder is defined here as a tool holder highly integrated with smart sensor device, which diagram is as shown in the left part of Fig. 1. The smart sensor device is internally or externally integrated with the tool holder. In order to guarantee that the integrated sensor device would not ruin the dynamic balance of the tool and tool holder, the smart sensor device should be integrated meticulously and symmetrically in relative to the rotating center of the tool or holder. The developed smart holder is able to acquire the frequency domain and time domain information via integrated accelerometer with enough frequency band and magnitude range.

2.2   Wireless Network

Table 1. Comparison of wireless technologies dedicated to IoT

Name	Bluetooth	NB-IoT	LoRa	Zigbee	Wi-Fi	Sigfox
Data Throughput	Up to 2 Mbps	Up to 1 Mbps	Up to 50 Kbps	Up to 250 Kbps	Up to 100 Mbps	Up to 0.1 Kbps
Transmit Power	−18–8 dBm	14 dBm	20 dBm	8–10 dBm	23 dBm	14 dBm
Cover Range	50–150 m	164 dB	2–5 km urban, 10–15 km rural	Up to 1000 m	Up to 100 m	3–10 km urban, 20–50 km rural
Topology	Star/Mesh	Star	Star	Mesh/Star	Star	Star
IP at the Device Node	No	Yes	No	No	Yes	No

The smart holder spins at very high speed with spindle, e.g., 3000–80000 rpm, which makes wireless connection for data transmission preferable. However, independent power supply system requires the smart holder consume as less power as possible. In this research work, the wireless network is divided into two levels: Level-1 and Level-2. Level-1 is defined as the wireless network from the terminal devices to the wireless edge gateway. Level-2 is defined as the wireless network from the wireless edge gateway to the CNC edge server. In order to guarantee that the smart holder which is an independent power supply system can work with CNC as loog as possible, the power consumption of the radio-on-chip is required to be as low as possible. Meanwhile, the employed radio-on-chip is also required to support high data rate transmission. In the end-mill conditions monitoring system, the bandwidth of smart sensor is highly required 15 KHz at least. For the acceleration sensor with triple perpendicular accelerometers, 720Kbits data are generated per second, which means the wireless radio link should support 720 Kbps data rate at least. Table 1 summarizes several typical IoT wireless technologies from multiple aspects. BLE, NB-IoT and Wi-Fi can meet the demand of data rate while only the BLE meets the demand of low power consumption. LoRa, Zigbee and Sigfox are low-power-consumption wireless technologies but they can't support high data rate, like 720 Kbps. In the industrial environment, 50–150 m cover range provided by BLE can also meet the communication distance demand. One BLE master can accommodate 6 BLE slaves for accessing. Therefore, the BLE is selected as the Level-1 wireless technology in this system design.

2.3 CNC Edge Server

CNC edge server stores the acquired raw data in which conditions related information of end-mill is potentially contained. With powerful ability of computing, the CNC edge server can support the implementations of data extraction and data mining algorithms. The data mining algorithm explores the extracted data and outputs the decision of end-mill conditions in real time. The data extraction and data mining will be elaborated in Sects. 3 and 4 respectively.

3   Data Extraction

During the whole cutting process, data extraction performs continually without interruption. The cutting process includes a certain number of periodical operations as shown in Fig. 3. Each periodical operation as shown in Fig. 3 includes: ① pulling down, ② feeding in, ③ cutting, ④ feeding out, ⑤ pulling up, ⑥ returning and ⑦ forwarding, which means the data acquired from the machine often contains contributions from several different components as well as noise. However, the data acquired by the smart sensor device only during the ③ cutting period contains the desired vibration information. That means the data acquired during pulling down, feeding in, feeding out, pulling up, forwarding covers no meaningful information about the condition of end-mill and possibly become noise. Therefore, one of the major challenges of condition monitoring is how to point out the signal content that is hightly related to the state of the desired monitoring end-mill. In order to extract the desired data and improve the accuracy of data mining, it is highly necessary to figure out the start point and end point of each periodical cutting process in the acquired data.

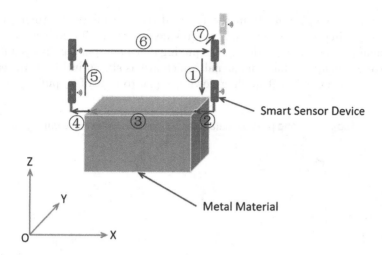

Fig. 3. Anatomy of one periodical operation of the whole working process.

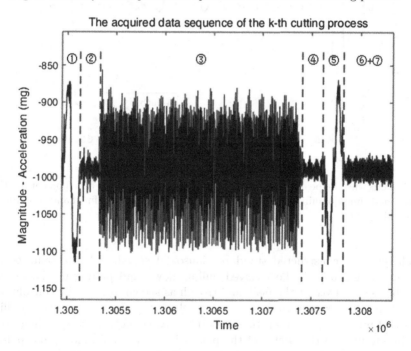

Fig. 4. Signal anatomy of the k-th working process.

Representing the received digital time domain signal from the smart sensor device as $x(n), n \in [1, \infty)$ and n is integer. Assuming the k-th cutting period signal as $x(n), n \in [n_{k,s}, n_{k,e}]$, where $n_{k,s}$ and $n_{k,e}$ represent the start point and end point of the k-th cutting process. However, we find that it is hard to figure out the $n_{k,s}$ and $n_{k,e}$ only from the received data sequence. Fortunately, the actions of pulling down and pulling up provide us very useful information. The time domain signal acquired during the pulling down and pulling up is similar to a positive or negative sinusoidal signal, which are as shown in Fig. 4. In reality, the period time of action ① pulling down is equal to that of ⑤ pulling up.

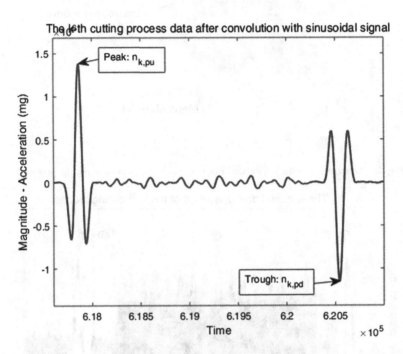

Fig. 5. Detecting the peak and trough of the k-th cutting process based on convoluting the acquired time-domain vibration data sequence with the predefined and constructed sinusoidal signal.

Therefore, a constructed standard sinusoidal signal with the same period time and magnitude as the received pulling down and pulling up data signal could be used to extract the peak and trough as shown in Fig. 5 by convolution. The extracted peaks and troughs are very helpful to detect the events of pulling down and pulling up. The cutting period is located between the pulling down and pulling up and the center of the period between pulling down and pulling up is the same as the center of cutting period. According to the detected peak location and the detected trough location, the center location can be determined. Assuming that the location of the trough is at $n_{k,pd}$ in time domain and that of the peak is at $n_{k,pu}$, the center location can be calculated by

$$n_{k,c} = \frac{n_{k,pd} + n_{k,pu}}{2} \tag{1}$$

The period of the constructed standard sinusoidal signal can be determined by previous experiments, which is represented by ℓ_{sin}. Normally, the feeding speed of the holder is constant. Therefore, the cutting period can be calculated by

$$\ell_{k,cutting} = (n_{k,pu} - n_{k,pd} - \ell_{sin})\frac{L_{c,m}}{L_{fi,m} + L_{c,m} + L_{fo,m}} \tag{2}$$

where $L_{c,m}$ is the measured physical length of the to be cutted metal material, $L_{fi,m}$ and $L_{fo,m}$ represent the measured physical length of the feeding in and feeding out procedure. Based on these, the start point $n_{k,s}$ and end point $n_{k,e}$ of the k-th cutting process can be obtained by

$$n_{k,s} = n_{k,c} - \frac{\ell_{k,cutting}}{2} \tag{3}$$

$$n_{k,e} = n_{k,c} + \frac{\ell_{k,cutting}}{2} \tag{4}$$

Based on the detection of the starting point and ending point of the k-th cutting process, the k-th desired data $x_n, n \in [n_{k,s}, n_{k,e}]$ containing the potential information highly related to the condition of end-mill can be obtained.

4 Data Mining

The desired data sequence has be obtained in the Sect. 3. This section will dig the potential information highly related to the conditions of end-mill and further decide the conditions of end-mill. Based on damage level, the conditions of end-mill can be divided into four types: no damage, low damage, medium damage and high damage. Theoretically, the magnitude of vibration induced by the friction between tool tip and workpiece is proportional to the damage level.

Data mining functions as transforming the original data into useful features to accomplish conditions detection. Sensors are used for advanced machine monitoring [12]. The cutting force, cutting temperature, shocking frequency, shocking magnitude, acoustic, motor power or current are generally important to evaluate the condition of the end-mill. Tool wear increases the friction between the cutting lips and surrounding workpiece material, which consequently leads to the increase of cutting force and temperature [6]. Torque and cutting forces are considered as the detection information to provide assessment of the tool condition since the cutting force is proportional to the friction between tool lips and workpiece material [7,8,11]. The current or power information of the motor is explored to online condition monitoring in [9,10]. The work [13], covering indirect monitoring methods such as force, vibration and current measurement, summarized the monitoring methods, including signal analysis and diagnostic techniques for tool wear monitoring and gave a comparison. Acoustic emission (AE) signals acquired during machining is explored for tool conditions monitoring [16]. Part of the typical research work are summarized as in Table 2.

Table 2. Methods of conditions monitoring of end-mill based on different sensors

Sensor	Related research work
Cutting force	Jantunen et al. [13], Klaic et al. [6], Ertunc et al. [7], Lin et al. [8], Subramanian et al. [11]
Cutting temperature	Shindou et al. [1], Kodama et al. [5], Klaic et al. [6]
Vibration frequency	Zhang et al. [2], Julie et al. [3], Jantunen et al. [13], Cuka et al. [18]
Vibration magnitude	Zhang et al. [2], Julie et al. [3], Cuka et al. [18]
Acoustic emission (AE)	Ravindra et al. [16]
Motor power or current	Franco-Gasca et al. [9], Xiaoli et al. [10], Jantunen et al. [13]

As we can see, lots of research works on data mining algorithm, such as machine learning decision trees [6], decision fusion based on hidden markov model [13] and decision fusion [14], back propagation wavelet neural network [15], infrared thermography technology [1], finite element analysis (FEA) [17], dedicated to the condition monitoring of end-mill have been proposed and developed. Therefore, we will focus on system level design and demonstration rather than data-mining algorithm development in this research work. Even though, the others developed data-mining algorithms can also be implemented on our developed CNC edge server for practical applications.

In order to demonstrate the whole system, statistical *Root Mean Square* (RMS), a simple but efficient and practical feature extraction algorithm is employed in this developed prototype. For the k-th desired data $x_n, n \in [n_{k,s}, n_{k,e}]$ of the k-th cutting process, the corresponding k-th RMS value can be calculated as

$$x_{rms,k} = \sqrt{\frac{\sum_{n=n_{k,s}}^{n_{k,e}} (x_n - x_{0,k})^2}{n_{k,e} - n_{k,s}}} \tag{5}$$

where $x_{0,k} := \frac{\sum_{n=n_{k,s}}^{n_{k,e}} x_n}{n_{k,e} - n_{k,s}}$ represents the mean vibration magnitude value of the k-th cutting process.

We found that the second-order RMS values can extract deeper features and consequently more obviously evaluate the conditions of end-mill. In this paper, we define the second-order RMS as following:

$$x_{rms^2,K} = \sqrt{\frac{\sum_{k=K_s}^{K_e} (x_{rms,k} - x_{0,rms,k})^2}{K_e - K_s}} \tag{6}$$

where K represents the K-th cutting layer of the workpiece material and $x_{0,rms,k} := \frac{\sum_{k=K_s}^{K_e} x_{rms,k}}{K_e - K_s}$ in which K_s and K_e represent the first RMS value and last RMS value of the K-th cutting layer respectively.

5   Experimental Results

The measurements of the vibration magnitude of the tool holder induced by cutting force are made by using a smart holder which is highly integrated with a tri-axial accelerometer. In this experiment, Bosch BMA280 is chosen as the integrated accelerometer and the experimental setup is specified as in Table 3.

Table 3. Experimental setup

Tool type	Spindle speed	Feeding force	Depth of cut AP	Width of cut AE
D6R0.3	6500 rpm	500	0.05 mm	0.2 mm

The first-order RMS values of the whole cutting process is as shown in Fig. 6, in which $x_{rms,x}$, $x_{rms,y}$ and $x_{rms,z}$ represent the RMS value of the vibration magnitude in the X direction, Y direction and Z direction respectively. As it can be seen in Fig. 6, the fluctuation of vibration magnitude induced by the cutting friction between end-mill and workpiece become more and more serious, especially in the X and Y directions.

The second-order RMS values of the whole cutting process is as shown in Fig. 7, in which $x_{rms^2,x}$, $x_{rms^2,y}$ and $x_{rms^2,z}$ represent the second order RMS value of the vibration magnitude in the X direction, Y direction and Z direction respectively. Compared to the Fig. 6, the Fig. 7 can reflect more clearly the

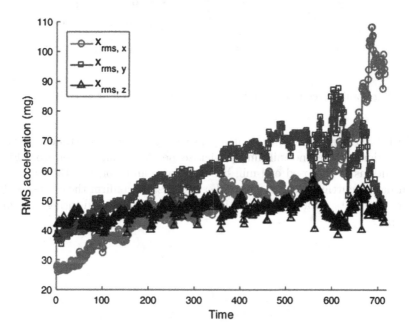

Fig. 6. The RMS of acceleration magnitude.

conditions of the end-mill. As the cutting process going on, the second order RMS values of the vibration magnitude will go to small but with fluctuation, which means the end-mill is under low damage. While as the cutting continue, the damage level of the end-mill will go into medium damage. Under medium damage, the second order values become bigger due to that the friction between the end-mill and the work piece is bigger. When the end-mill is under high damage, the slope of the second order values line become smaller compared to that of the medium damage, which is shown as in Fig. 7.

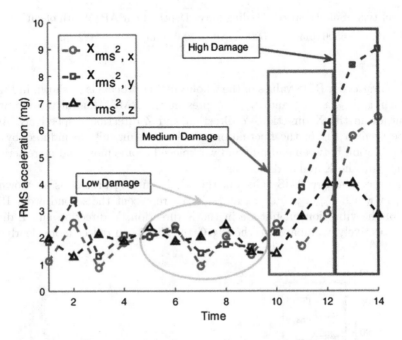

Fig. 7. The second-order RMS values of the acceleration magnitude.

During the experiment, the cutting process is temporary stoped to watch the conditions of the end-mill under microscope. As it can be seen from Fig. 8, the conditions of the used end-mill become worse and worse as the time going on during the cutting process. These observed results confirm the corresponding monitored results obtained by the developed conditions monitoring system in this paper.

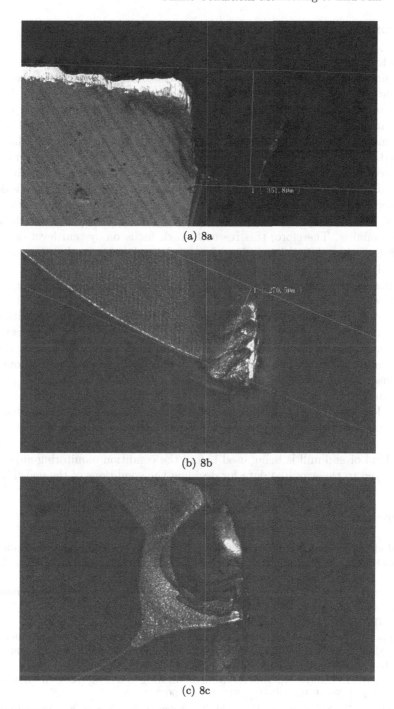

Fig. 8. The photos of the tips conditions under microscope with 500 times magnifying. (a) shows low damage of used end-mill; (b) shows medium damage of the used end-mill; (c) shows high damage of the used end-mill.

6   Conclusions and Future Work

End-mill included CNCs have been widely employed in factories for high precision manufacturing. Current end-mill conditions monitoring systems lack efficient and effective fault diagnosis and prediction. In this paper, a tool holder highly integrated with tri-axial accelerometer and auxiliary electronic equipments, namely smart holder, is elaborately developed. The developed smart holder makes almost no contributions to the system dynamic balance. The data acquired from the smart holder often contains contributions from several different components as well as noise. Therefore, a data-extraction algorithm is proposed in this research work to purely extract the real needed cutting data. The proposed second-order RMS algorithm is employed here to detect the features of the extracted data sequence. In fact, there are lots of research work on data mining. Therefore, this research work focus on system level development rather than data mining algorithms and emphasizes on the practical and potential commercial deployment.

Depending on different materials or different diameter, the end-mills could be different, which leads the conditions monitoring system to be much more complicated. In instinct, we can not use one conditions monitoring algorithm to all different kind of end-mills. Therefore in the CNC server, there should exist a algorithm list which is corresponding a end-mill list. Ideally, each specific conditions monitoring algorithm corresponds to a specific kind of end-mill. However, the knowledge of the being used end-mill is not available at the CNC server. Consequently, the most suitable conditions monitoring algorithm for the being used end-mill can not be chosen exactly. To solve this problem, more advanced technology like machine learning will be developed to classify different types of end-mill in the prospective. That means deep learning network will decide which kind of end-mill is being used before the condition monitoring algorithm is employed to the acquired data for deciding the conditions of the end-mill.

References

1. Shindou, M., Kodama, H., Hirogaki, T., Aoyama, E.: Monitoring of end-mill process based on infrared imagery with a high speed thermography. Key Eng. Mater. **625**, 213–218 (2015). J. Trans. Tech Pubulications
2. Zhang, C., Yao, X., Zhang, J., Jin, H.: Tool condition monitoring and remaining useful life prognostic based on a wireless sensor in dry milling operations. Sensors **16**, 795 (2016). https://doi.org/10.3390/s16060795
3. Zhang, J.Z., Chen, J.C.: Tool condition monitoring in an end-milling operation based on the vibration signal collected through a microcontroller-based acquisition system. Int. J. Adv. Manuf. Technol. **39**(1–2), 118–128 (2008)
4. Yesilyurt, I., Ozturk, H.: Tool condtion monitoring in milling using vibration analysis. Int. J. Prod. Res. **45**(4), 1013–1028 (2006)
5. Kodama, H., Shindou, M., Hirogaki, T., Aoyama, E., Ogawa, K.: An end-milling condition decision support system using data-mining for difficult-to-cut materials. Adv. Mater. Res. **565**, 472–477 (2012)

6. Klaic, M., Staroveski, T., Udiljak, T.: Tool wear classification using decision trees in stone drilling applications: a preliminary study. Procedia Eng. **69**, 1326–1335 (2014). 24th DAAAM International Symposium on Intelligent Manufacturing and Automation (2013)
7. Ertunc, H.M., Loparo, K.A.: A decision fusion algorithm for tool wear condition monitoring in drilling. Int. J. Mach. Tools Manuf. **41**(9), 1347–1362 (2001)
8. Lin, S.C., Ting, C.J.: Tool wear monitoring in drilling using force signals. Wear **180**(1–2), 53–60 (1995)
9. Franco-Gasca, L.A., Herrera-Ruiz, G., Peniche-Vera, R., de Jesús Romero-Troncoso, R., Leal-Tafolla, W.: Sensorless tool failure monitoring system for drilling machines. Int. J. Mach. Tools Manuf. **46**(3–4), 381–386 (2006)
10. Xiaoli, L.: On-line detection of the breakage of small diameter drills using current signature wavelet transform. Int. J. Mach. Tools Manuf. **39**(1), 157–164 (1999)
11. Subramanian, K., Cook, N.H.: Sensing of drill wear and prediction of drill life (I). J. Eng. Ind. Trans. ASME **99**(2), 295–301 (1977)
12. Teti, R., Jemielniak, K., O'Donnell, G., Dornfeld, D.: Advanced monitoring of machining operations. CIRP Ann. Manuf. Technol. **59**(2), 717–739 (2010)
13. Jantunen, E.: A summary of methods applied to tool condition monitoring in drilling. J. Mach. Tools Manuf. **42**(9), 997–1010 (2002)
14. Natarajan, U., Arun, P., Periasamy, V.M.: A decision fusion algorithm for tool condition monitoring in drilling using Hidden Markov Model (HMM). Indian J. Eng. Mater. Sci. **13**, 103–109 (2006)
15. Yang, X., Kumehara, H., Zhang, W.: Back propagation wavelet neural network based prediction of drill wear from thrust force and cutting torque signals. Comput. Inf. Sci. **2**(3), 75–86 (2009)
16. Ravindra, H.V., Srinivasa, Y.G., Krishnamurthy, R.: Acoustic emission for tool condtion monitoring in metal cutting. Wear **212**(1), 78–84 (1997)
17. Yen, Y.C., Sohner, J., Lilly, B., Altan, T.: Estimation of tool wear in orthogonal cutting using the finite element analysis. J. Mater. Process. Technol. **146**, 82–91 (2004)
18. Cuka, B., Kim, D.-W.: Fuzzy logic based tool condition monitoring for end-milling. Rob. Comput.-Integr. Manuf. **47**(C), 22–36 (2017)

Context-Aware Continuous Authentication and Dynamic Device Pairing for Enterprise IoT

Na Yu$^{(\boxtimes)}$, Jia Ma, Xudong Jin, Jian Wang, and Ken Chen

Samsung Research America, Mountain View, CA 94043, USA
nyuyuna@gmail.com,
{jia.ma,xudong.jin,jianl.w,geng.c}@samsung.com

Abstract. Enterprise IoT is an advanced extension of Internet of Things (IoT) that enables intelligent enterprise systems. It focuses on connecting the enterprise assets and their devices with backend application services and frontend user interactions. While it is more complicated and more impactful than smart home, it faces several challenges such as a large number of IoT devices deployed at various locations and also multiple users to be granted with different permissions. To solve these challenges, we propose a multi-domain enterprise IoT system in consideration of both user movement and IoT device relocation. We propose a context-aware continuous authentication method to authenticate mobile users to the IoT domains based on the context inferred from various sensors on the smartphones and in the IoT domains. We also propose a dynamic device pairing method to support the mobility of users and IoT devices based on data (e.g., contexts, access history, etc.) sharing among the IoT domain, the enterprise server, and the mobile users.

Keywords: Continuous authentication · Device pairing · Internet of Things

1 Introduction

Internet of Things (IoT) becomes increasingly helpful in people's daily life, with many smart devices interacting with the environment and communicating with other devices to provide seamless services such as security and climate control at home or in the workspace. Emerging IoT platforms also provide increasing functionality to enable the autonomous interactions between IoT devices and people. The IoT solutions are evolved from machine-to-machine (M2M) solutions which are focused on closed environment with limited connectivity and sensing/actuation solutions which automate the tasks. Integrating the existing solutions into the outside world is critical to provide full-fledged IoT solutions. However, different IoT solutions are needed for various application scenarios such as home automation and enterprise IoT. While it is difficult to standardize the solutions for all IoT platforms, it is relatively easy to focus on subnets of things such as in the enterprise environment. Enterprise IoT focuses on a class of assets with multiple devices from different vendors deployed on the assets. Enterprise IoT solution is an IT system that connects assets (i.e., a property that is

© Springer Nature Switzerland AG 2019
V. Issarny et al. (Eds.): ICIOT 2019, LNCS 11519, pp. 114–122, 2019.
https://doi.org/10.1007/978-3-030-23357-0_9

managed in order to generate revenue to help improve a company's operations) and their devices (include sensors and actuators deployed on the assets) with backend application services and frontend user interactions [1]. It is more complicated than smart home and would be even more valuable for research and development since enterprise IoT has a much bigger impact than home automation.

Enterprise IoT not only faces the challenges in a large number of devices which are deployed at various locations in the enterprise, but it also needs to authenticate multiple users with different permissions. Dynamically managing the IoT devices and automatically granting user accesses by scene are non-trivial. For example, a company may deploy IoT devices such as camera, smart plug, smart speaker, voice assistant, and robot vacuum in the meeting rooms and office spaces. An employee may be granted access to the IoT devices in his/her office and nearby meeting rooms. In order to access the enterprise IoT, the employee can use a handheld mobile device such as smartphone to connect to the enterprise WiFi and login with the enterprise server using employee credentials. However, for security and privacy considerations, the access permissions of an employee should be limited to a subset of IoT devices based on the employee's location and fine-grained location context such as in a meeting room, but not all the devices deployed in the entire enterprise IoT nor all the time. For the location context, since an employee usually needs to scan the employee badge to enter an office suite, it is reasonable to grant access to IoT devices based on location as the employee is already authenticated to enter this location. However, as employees are moving around in the company, autonomous and continuous authentication of mobile users to different subsets of IoT devices is a challenge. On the other hand, while an employee is moving (e.g., from a meeting room to another room), he/she may also move an IoT device (e.g., take a smart plug or a smart speaker to a different room for another meeting). As an IoT device may need to be paired with another IoT device to work together for some tasks (e.g., a smart plug or a smart speaker can be paired with a voice assist), dynamically pairing the IoT devices is yet another challenge in the mobile environment of enterprise IoT.

In this paper, we focus on solving the above challenges in enterprise IoT, i.e., how mobile users interact with IoT devices and how the IoT devices interact with each other. To match a mobile user with a relevant subset of IoT devices, we divide the enterprise IoT by IoT domains. Each domain contains relevant scenes, in which the IoT devices are paired to each other, and the mobile users (i.e., employees carrying smartphones connected to the enterprise WiFi and are authenticated to the enterprise server with employee credentials) located inside the IoT domain can be automatically granted access to the IoT devices in this IoT domain. We first propose the multi-domain enterprise IoT system architecture that contains devices with different roles. We then propose a context-aware continuous authentication method to authenticate mobile users to the IoT domains based on the context inferred from various sensors on the smartphones and in the IoT domains. We also propose a dynamic device pairing method for the IoT devices in case mobile users move the IoT devices across IoT domains. The proposed method will be based on data (e.g., contexts, access history, etc.) sharing among the IoT domains, the enterprise server, and the mobile users. We finally extend the work with learning-based device pairing and security analytic framework in the future work when the enterprise IoT data is available.

2   Related Work

Although IoT has been studied a lot in both academia and industry with various services and applications discussed, enterprise IoT has been ignored. There are very few research and development targeted at enterprise IoT environment. Researchers and engineers from Samsung have developed an IoT platform named Brightics-IoT which is targeting enterprise manufacturing sector [2, 3]. The key features of Brightics-IoT include device connectivity, device management, end to end security, data visualization, and IoT analytics. For device management, it points out that an IoT platform should support management of grouped devices and a single device by their business needs, but it does not consider the scenario that needs to dynamically pairing IoT devices upon movement. For end-to-end security, it focuses on IoT device authentication and the secure data pipeline from IoT devices to data processing services, but it does not consider user authentication to access the IoT devices. Different from the existing work presented in Brightics-IoT, we focus on the autonomous user authentication and dynamic device pairing problems in a mobile environment.

Beyond enterprise IoT, there are many existing works focused on user authentication and device pairing. State-of-the-art authentication methods often use multi-factor or multi-level authentication to verify the identity of a user or a device. The work in [4] proposes context-awareness as a method to enhance the authentication process in the industrial IoT, utilizing the fact that devices located in the same place consistently observe similar ambient context information. The work in [5] proposes a proximity-based device authentication mechanism which requires user to hold smartphone and perform one of two hand-gestures in front of IoT devices. The work in [6] proposes a technology that links a device's context to an activity's semantics using natural language process and program analysis for user-centric authorization. The work in [7] proposes a context-based permission system that provides contextual integrity by supporting fine-grained context identification for sensitive actions to help users perform effective access control. The work in [8] proposes a continuous authentication framework that integrates contextual information for user authentication in smart homes. The work in [9, 10] propose a context-based device pairing mechanism that uses time as the common factor across different sensor types, with a conversion of heterogeneous sensing signals into a common state-space to generate fingerprints for pairing. The above existing work are all focused on a single IoT domain (e.g., smart home). Although some of their methods can be applied in our work, we are more focused on the approaches for multi-domain enterprise IoT.

3   System Architecture

We propose a multi-domain enterprise IoT system that divides the enterprise IoT by IoT domains based on the relevant scenes such as an office suite or a meeting room. The IoT devices inside an IoT domain are paired to each other, and the mobile users located inside the IoT domain can be automatically granted access to the IoT devices. The system architecture as shown in Fig. 1 contains the following types of devices.

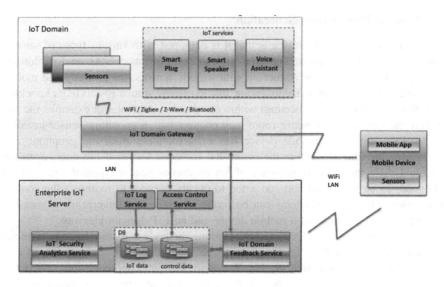

Fig. 1. System architecture

IoT Domain Gateway: A gateway has multi-modal communication capabilities (e.g., WiFi, ZigBee, Z-Wave, and Bluetooth) and can be configured for enterprise local network access. The gateway also has sensing capabilities. It either equips with common types of sensors (e.g., motion sensor, geophone, and microphone) or securely connects with separate sensors via the supported communication methods.

IoT Service Device: A service device is an end device which provides certain service, e.g., smart plug, smart speaker, and voice assistant. The service device can communicate with the gateway via one of the supported communication methods.

Enterprise IoT Server: An IoT server provides access control service and IoT log service for feedback and analysis, respectively. The IoT sever communicates with the IoT domain gateways via enterprise local area network.

Mobile Device: A mobile device refers to the user's smartphone. The mobile device can discover nearby IoT domain gateways via WiFi, then lookup their IP addresses in the enterprise local area network via the enterprise IoT server, and further authenticate and connect with the IoT domain gateways.

4 Context-Aware Continuous Authentication

During a mobile user's (employee) stay in the enterprise, his/her mobile device is required to connect in the enterprise WiFi network or via VPN in order to access the enterprise IoT domains. We adopt the fact that devices located in the same place consistently observe similar ambient context information [4] to continuously authenticate the mobile user with IoT domain gateways in an autonomous and dynamic way.

4.1   Context Fingerprints Generation

The advantage of a mobile device is that it is equipped with various types of sensors which are capable to capture the ambient context information. As an IoT domain gateway is also equipped or connected with various sensors, the gateway and mobile device present in the same IoT domain are able to capture similar events (e.g., knocking at the door or speaking in a meeting) within certain time interval. For example, the IoT domain gateway in a conference room may connect with a geophone sensor installed on the door, while the mobile device has a microphone. Both the geophone and microphone are able to capture the event that someone knock at the door, open the door, and close the door. In presence of heterogeneous sensor types, the raw sensor data needs to be processed and converted to events in order to represent the context information. The captured events can be further converted to fingerprints to measure the co-presence similarity of a mobile device and an IoT domain gateway.

Existing work has leveraged machine learning methods to extract features from the raw sensor data, cluster the features into events, and generate fingerprint bits to represent the context information [9, 10]. We adopt the same approach for context fingerprints generation while focus on the continuous authentication problem. The problem we try to solve includes how to match the mobile device with the co-present IoT domain gateways based on the context fingerprints, how to continuously authenticate the mobile device across the IoT domains, and how to deal with the context switch.

4.2   Co-presence Authentication Algorithm

IoT domain gateways are stationary, so they can capture the entire events happening in the domain over time. In contrast, mobile devices move across the IoT domains, so they capture events in different domains and may miss or mix part of the events when crossing the boundaries. We use the event timeline of IoT domain gateways as the baseline and match the events of mobile device using an adaptive window that covers the length of event fingerprint bits (in Algorithm 1), so time synchronization is not required.

For example, mobile device U1 and gateways G1-G4 run a co-presence authentication algorithm (Algorithm 1) together that covers the following scenarios (in Fig. 2):

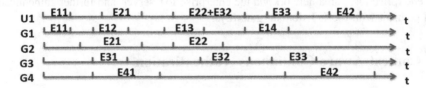

Fig. 2. Sample event timeline

(1) U1 enters the region of G1 with a full event E11 captured (U1 authenticates with G1); (2) U1 enters G2 with a partial event E21 (U1 authenticates with G2 if the

partial E21 has enough fingerprint bits); (3) U1 enters G3 with a mix of E22 and E32 (U1 may authenticates with G2 and G3 at the same time if both have enough fingerprint bits); (4) U1 enters and exits G4 with a short interval of event E42 (U1 may not authenticate with G4 if the partial E42 does not have enough fingerprint bits).

Alg. 1. Co-presence authentication algorithm

[Mobile device side]

Input: authentication period Pa, fingerprint bits min length Ln and max length Lm

Output: the authenticated list of co-presence gateways

1: Set periodic timer Ta with interval Pa;

2: Continuously generates fingerprint bits when events are captured;

3: On timer Ta expires or the fingerprint bits of a new event reaches Ln length:

4:     **If** exist fingerprint bits Fu with at least Ln length:

5:         Discover IoT domain gateways and send the last Lm bits of Fu to them;

6:     **For** each IoT domain gateway Gi with positive authentication decision:

7:         **If** Gi is not in the existing authenticated gateway list:

8:             Add Gi to the authenticated gateway list and connect to Gi;

9:     **For** each IoT domain gateway Gj with negative authentication decision:

10:         **If** Gj is in the existing authenticated gateway list:

11:             Disconnect from Gj and remove it from the authenticated gateway list;

12:     Reset timer Ta;

13: **Else if** timer Ta expires:

14:     Disconnect from all gateways in the list and clear the list;

[IoT domain gateway side]

Input: window length factor fw ($>=1.0$), similarity threshold THs (<1.0)

Output: authentication decision

1: Continuously generates fingerprint bits when events are captured;

2: On fingerprint bits Fu with length Lx is received from mobile user Ux:

3:     Compute the minimum edit distance (Dn) of Fu in the local fingerprint bits within the window length of $fw*Lx$;

4:     **If** the matching ratio ($1- Dn/Lx$) exceeds the similarity threshold THs:

5:         Send authentication decision true to Ux and store the decision;

6:     **Else**:

7:         Send authentication decision false to Ux and store the decision;

5 Dynamic Device Pairing

5.1 Dynamic Device Paring Algorithm

An IoT service device may not have the sensors to capture context information as a mobile device does, so we need to utilize the historic data from the server for collaboration. When mobile device U1 connects with gateway G1 and accesses IoT service devices D1 and D2, the enterprise IoT server receives a series of control data: (1) U1 connects G1; (2) U1 accesses D1; (3) U1 accesses D2; (4) U1 disconnects G1.

When U1 moves to another IoT domain and connects with gateway G2, U1 may carry a previous accessed IoT service device D1 to the new IoT domain. When U1 connects to G2, G2 needs to determine whether there is a relocation of IoT service device and automatically pair with a relocated device using the following steps:

(1) G2 pulls the control data history of U1 from the enterprise IoT server when U1 requests to connect. The control data of U1 reveals the previously connected gateway G1 and previously accessed devices D1 and D2. (2) G2 further pulls the control data history of D1 and D2, containing the pairing status with the gateways and also the wireless signal strength. There are several possible ground truths of D1 or D2: (a) It is still paired with G1 and is not moved; (b) it is still paired with G1 but actually moved; (c) it is not paired with G1 since it is actually moved; (d) it is not paired with G1 even it is not moved. (3) G2 runs a dynamic pairing algorithm (Algorithm 2) to classify the ground truth and make pairing decision for D1 and D2, respectively.

Alg. 2. Dynamic pairing algorithm
Input: IoT service device Dy, control data history of Dy
Output: feedback to server or request to mobile user U1, pairing decision
1: G2 discovers IoT service devices;
2: **If** Dy in the discovery results:
3:    **If** Dy is not paired with any gateway:
4:       Send feedback "Dy is possible moved to G2" to server;
5:       Return pairing decision true and pair with Dy;
6:    **Else if** Dy is paired with G1:
7:       Compare the wireless signal strength pattern of Dy towards G2 versus G1;
8:       **If** the pattern shows increasing towards G2 while decreasing towards G1:
9:          Send feedback "Dy is possible moved to G2" to server;
10:          Return pairing decision true and pair with Dy;
11:       **Else if** the pattern shows stable signal strength towards both G2 and G1:
12:          Return pairing decision false;
13:       **Else:**
14:          Send request "Please confirm if you moved Dy" to mobile user U1;
15:          **If** receive positive response from U1:
16:             Send feedback "Dy is possible moved to G2" to server;
17:             Return pairing decision true and pair with Dy;
18:          **Else:**
19:             Return pairing decision false;
20:    **Else:**
21:       Return pairing decision false;
22: **Else:**
23:    **If** Dy is not paired with any gateway:
24:       Send feedback "Dy is possible offline" to server;
25:       Return pairing decision false;

5.2 IoT Domain Feedback

The dynamic pairing algorithm outputs not only the pairing decision, but also the feedback to the enterprise IoT server. The feedback incorporating the ground truth can be used to train a pairing classifier or a learning model to help improve the pairing decision strategy and reduce the request to the mobile users. The trained classifier or model can be pushed to the IoT domain gateways to update the pairing algorithm.

The pairing classifier or learning model can be trained with a specific enterprise environment. It is highly relevant to the office layouts, device deployment (distance between devices and signal attenuation through walls), and employee activity patterns. Training the classifier or model based on the employee activity patterns can help reducing user interactions. Further, the trained classifier or model only works in the specific enterprise environment, so it can prevent threats from outside attackers who try to use typical models to predict the behaviors of the enterprise IoT.

6 Conclusions and Future Work

In this paper, we have proposed the system and methods of context-aware continuous authentication and dynamic device pairing for multi-domain enterprise IoT in consideration of both user movement and IoT device relocation. As an ongoing work, we plan to develop a prototype system using Samsung Galaxy S10 smartphone and Samsung SmartThings IoT platform. We will evaluate the proposed algorithms based on the prototype system and present the results in the future work. Further, we will collect both IoT data (sensor data and device actions) and control data (device pairing and user operations) from the prototype system. The collected data will be used to improve the system and also provide security features. For example, a learning-based device pairing method can be developed based on the collected data. We can utilize machine learning models to reduce the human in the loop operations and achieve more autonomous decisions on device pairing. In addition, we can also build a security analytic framework to identify context leakage for potential attacks.

References

1. Slama, D., Puhlmann, F., Morrish, J., Bhatnagar, R.: Enterprise IoT. O'Reilly Media Inc., Sebastopol (2015)
2. Choi, H.: Brightics-IoT: key attractive features of enterprise targeted IoT platform. In: IEEE International Conference on Industrial Internet (2018). [Demo]
3. Choi, H., Song, J., Yi, K.: Brightics-IoT: towards effective industrial IoT platforms for connected smart factories. In: IEEE International Conference on Industrial Internet (2018)
4. Rothe, L., Loske., M., Gertler, D.: proposing context-aware authentication for the industrial internet of things. In: IEEE Global Conference on Internet of Things (2018)
5. Zhang, J., Wang, Z., Yang, Z., Zhang, Q.: Proximity based IoT device authentication. In: IEEE Conference on Computer Communications (2017)
6. Tian, Y., et al.: SmartAuth: user-centered authorization for the internet of things. In: USENIX Security Symposium (2017)

7. Jia, Y., et al.: Context IoT: towards providing contextual integrity to applied IoT platforms. In: The Network and Distributed System Security Symposium (2017)
8. Ashibani, Y., Kauling, D., Mahmoud, Q.: Design and Implementation of a contextual-based continuous authentication framework for smart homes. Appl. Syst. Innov. **2**, 4 (2019)
9. Han, J., et al.: Do you feel what i hear? Enabling autonomous IoT device pairing using different sensor types. In: Symposium on Security and Privacy (2018)
10. Pan, S., et al.: UniverSense: IoT device pairing through heterogeneous sensing signals. In: International Workshop on Mobile Computing Systems and Applications (2018)

Smart IoT In-Car Life Detector System to Prevent Car Deaths

Nesreen Alsbou$^{(\boxtimes)}$, Ka Hei Samuel Chan, and Mohamed Afify

University of Central Oklahoma, Edmond, OK 73034, USA
nalsbou@uco.edu

Abstract. Unfortunately, many deaths are reported every year during the summer for infants, kids and pets who were left in cars and suffered from heatstroke. This paper is proposing a simple smart IoT system for in car detection of a living subject and taking the necessary actions to prevent their life loss. The system has a wide range of sensors including microwave sensors to collect a large set of data inside the car. The system will analyze the data and make the appropriate actions to prevent any death. These actions include sending an alert message to the parents and the emergency department, rolling down the windows, or starting the engine and turning on the air conditioner.

Keywords: Internet of Things (IoT) · Tree decision algorithm · Microwave · Passive infrared

1 Introduction

To prevent the number of deaths due to children being trapped in hot vehicles, an IoT life detector system is proposed in this paper. Since 1998, 37 children were killed by heatstroke per year in the United States [1]. An infant could experience un- compensable heat within 20 min, heatstroke within 105 min, and death in 125 min [2]. The heating rates of the interior of an economy car and a minivan under the sun are approximately 0.42 °C per minute and 0.30 °C per minute, respectively [3]. By detecting lives in a dangerous environment, alerting the parent and nearby emergency departments for rescue and/or acting on the vehicle, lives could be saved.

In literature, many papers discussed the detection of human lives in different situations. For example the authors in [4] used microwave sensors at 1150 MHz (L band, 1–2 GHz) to search for live people under earthquake rubble by detecting their heartbeats using the Doppler Effect. Another paper [5] discussed how they used microwaves to detect living beings by considering the movement of the rescue team around the disaster field, their microwave generator and antenna set up are similar, but they compare the feedback signals from two antennas by cross-correlation in frequency domain to eliminate the error made by the movement of the rescue team. A dynamic comprehensive model was developed in [6] to predict the rate of change in cabin temperature. They considered three main parameters; air temperature, global radiation, and wind velocity.

In this paper, rather than relying on a single sensor or situation, we will discuss how to enhance the accuracy of detecting a living being in a car. First, to detect a human life

---

The original version of this chapter was revised: an author's surname was corrected to "Chan". The correction to this chapter is available at https://doi.org/10.1007/978-3-030-23357-0_12

V. Issarny et al. (Eds.): ICIOT 2019, LNCS 11519, pp. 123–130, 2019.
https://doi.org/10.1007/978-3-030-23357-0_10

trapped in a car we can't use cameras inside the car to protect the privacy of the driver. Therefore, we need an alternative method. We can utilize carbon dioxide sensor, temperature sensor, microwave and passive infrared sensors to detect if the subject in the back seat is a life. Second, we can utilize smart devices and the cloud to alert parents and rescuing departments if there is a life in danger. Third, we can integrate our proposed system with the car controlling system or the Engine Control Unit (ECU) of the vehicle to take any life-saving actions such as rolling down the windows, starting the engine or turning on the air conditioner. The paper will introduce the overall idea of the smart system using microwave and passive infrared sensors and it will introduce the tree decision algorithm to send the data to the cloud. The paper will introduce the event engine system in the cloud platform that will send the alerts to the parents and the emergency department.

2   Overall System

As shown in Fig. 1 the smart IoT life detector will be implemented with four sensors: temperature sensor, CO2 sensor and two motion sensors. The sensors will monitor the atmosphere inside the car and the presence of a person inside the car. An algorithm will link between the threshold value and the human presence. We first conducted the experiment by testing each individual sensor. We then simulate an enclosed room with volume of 3000 L to replicate an enclosed car cabin. We tested our system by ourselves. If any reading went off, the system will send an alert through the cloud server and will contact the ECU unit of the vehicle to roll down the windows if necessary.

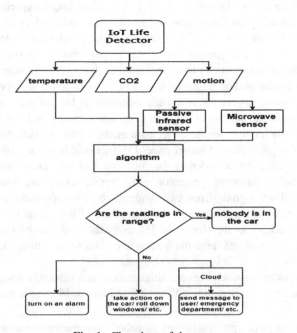

Fig. 1. Flowchart of the system

The Main system that will control the sensors will be a low power Microcontroller (MC) atmega328 that will be monitoring the readings of only one sensor and when one has an active situation it will set up an interrupt service to operate the other sensors. The sensors will be a PIR, Integrated Microwave Sensor, Temperature sensors, and SprintIR wide range low power CO2 Sensor.

A FLORA GPRS module will be receiving the emergency data and send it to the cloud application to alert the parents of a child detection in the car and a possible dangerous situation.

3   Critical Life Indicator

To distinguish between a life child and any other object placed on the backseat; we utilize sensors to make the classification. The device will have an algorithm with combination of data set that includes temperature, carbon dioxide, sound, and motion. If any reading went off, plus a life was detected, that life was in danger. Since some infants can stay silent for a long time, a combination of sensors is used to determine if there is an infant placed in the backseat. A simple algorithm can be set as if all data are in range, no life is trapped. For more accuracy of life detection, a combination of different sensor readings should be considered such as CO2, sound, and motion sensors. A temperature sensor is important too for an alert of critical temperature levels.

3.1   Temperature

An infant could experience un-compensable heat within 20 min, heat stroke within 105 min, and death in 125 min [2]. The heating rate, P of the interior of an economy car and a minivan under the sun are approximately 0.42 °C per minute and 0.30 °C per minute respectively [5].

$$T_{interior} = T_{initial} + P * t \, (^{\circ}\text{C}) \qquad (1)$$

Assuming room temperature is 25 °C, using Eq. 1 if an infant is placed in the backseat of a sedan, it would take 29 min to heat up the interior temperature of the car to the normal body temperature (37 °C). This means that heat will start flowing into the body in 29 min.

3.2   Carbon Dioxide

According to [6], above 1,000 ppm CO2 in air is associated with complaints of drowsiness and poor air. Between 2000 ppm to 5000 ppm, human will experience headache, sleepiness, stagnant, stale, and stuffy air. Above 5,000 ppm, toxicity or oxygen deprivation could occur. In our research, we assume the rate of carbon dioxide emission is constant, every breath out contains 4.0–5.3% of volume of carbon dioxide [7]. The average size of sedan has about 2800 L air and the Tidal volume (which is defined as the quantity of gas delivered with each breath) of a child is approximately 6 mL/kg and the respiratory rate of an infant is 30–60 breath per minute [8–10].

$$V_{CO2} = \frac{V_{tidal} * W_{infant} * R_{respiratory} * V_{\%,CO2emission}}{V_{vehicle}} * 10^6 (ppm) \qquad (2)$$

From Eq. 2, assuming tidal volume of an infant is 6 mL/kg, weighs 10 kg, s/he breathes 30 times per minute, 5% carbon dioxide every exhale volume, and vehicle volume is 2800 L, the infant is adding 32.1 ppm of carbon dioxide. It would take about 31 min for the child to feel drowsy and 62 min to experience headache and sleepiness.

4   Motion Detection

Human motion could be detected by passive infrared sensor and microwave sensor. To ensure a moving object or a life is monitored, an algorithm of combination of sensors could be used. The PIR senor will be monitoring the car atmosphere at all times and will be sending to the Microcontroller unit (MC) the date to detect the presence of a human body inside the car. If the threshold of danger zone is reached the microwave sensor will be reading the body motion inside the car, as the microwave sensor has a high sensitivity of motion sensing to make sure that a human being is detected in the backseat of the car.

4.1   Passive Infrared Sensor

An integrated circuit is used to detect any object that emits infrared radiation, its algorithm returns a value of high voltage if there is an object moving. The sensor will be taking readings at a rate of 10 Hz. If it has an active reading of human presence it will operate the other three sensors to recheck the danger zone of the threshold.

4.2   Microwave Sensor

We will be using a sensor called HB100 microwave module, which is using Doppler Effect to determine the speed of an object. It emits a constant 10.525 GHz microwave, then receives a reflected signal and analyzes its frequency to determine the speed of an object. This microwave sensor is operated with a low-pass amplifier circuit. From the sensor response, we can calculate the respiratory rate of a life, it detects a movement of a surface, in our case, the chest skin.

5   Internet of Things (IoT) System IoT System

The IoT system is handling the safety control which connects between the embedded system in the car and the Internet application services that alert the parents and the police department. The system is using the GPRS module to transmit data sent through the transmitter and receiver serial cable from the main system. The Module is transmitting data using the MQTT protocol to the cloud. The module is using a simple tree decision algorithm with two integers. Integer 1 represents a critical condition is detected and the system must be triggered/activated and an integer 0 represents a normal situation with all sensor values being less than the threshold values. The integer values are updated periodically and sent to the cloud server.

The algorithm makes a decision of activating the system by using Iterative Dichotomiser 3 (ID3) which uses entropy function and information gain as metrics. In Eq. 3, the entropy H(s) is the amount of the uncertainty in the data, s is the current set for which entropy is calculated and c is the set of classes we are choosing which is yes and no. If the values are under the threshold, the entropy will equal zero and if it is high it will equal 1. In Eq. 4, the E(Y, N) is the information gain which will be measuring the difference in the entropy H(s) before and after the set N is split with the set Y. As shown, N is the subsets created from splitting N by Y.

The algorithm will compute the entropy for the sensors values. For every attribute, the entropy is calculated, then we take the average of the information entropy, calculate the gain for the current attribute and pick the highest gain and then repeat. Based on the highest gain it will give a decision of yes or no and convert it to the integer values 0 and 1, respectively. The integer values are sent to the cloud server.

$$H(s) = \sum_{i=1}^{c} -T_i log_2 T_i \tag{3}$$

$$E(Y,N) = H(s) - \sum_{i \in N} T(i)H(i) \tag{4}$$

Figure 2 shows the cloud server has an event engine trigger with an active event window, the developer can set a threshold line to that window and if the value data exceeds the threshold it will send an alert.

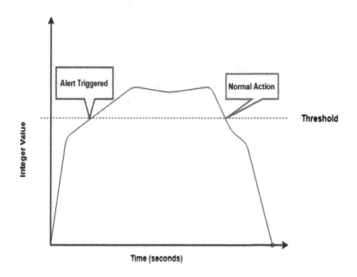

Fig. 2. Engine trigger events

The type of alert will depend on the time it took the value to cut the threshold, during the first 10 min it will send a text Message to the parents. After that period, it will send a recorded call to the emergency. To setup an automatic alert text message to be sent by the smart system for an alert, we designed an application with an action using a HTTP context value and assigned the context, device label and the variable ID, then a text message will be sent as shown in Fig. 3.

Fig. 3. Alert message system

6   Results

The designed system was tested partially and it was successful in detecting a human presence using the PIR sensor as shown in Fig. 4. Once a motion was detected, the system was activated to start checking all the sensor data and analyze them for any possible life threatening situation inside the car.

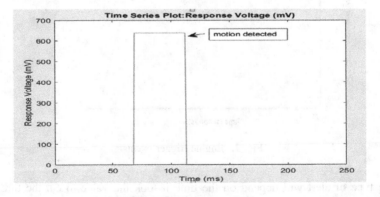

Fig. 4. PIR sensor results

The microwave sensor will be detecting the human motion in the car and insure the presence of a child before sending an alert message to the emergency department. Figure 5 shows a motion is detected within a range of time and thus the system will react to this movement inside the car. We processed the raw signal, then analyzed it with Fourier Transform. We can get the Respiratory rate at 0.22 Hz, i.e. 13.2 breathe per minute. The algorithm will send an alert after detecting motion for 30 s, an integer of a byte value of 1 will be sent over the wireless serial communication. The Server system will use the trigger engine to make an action event and send an alert through a text message to the parents and then the emergency department through a recorded voice call.

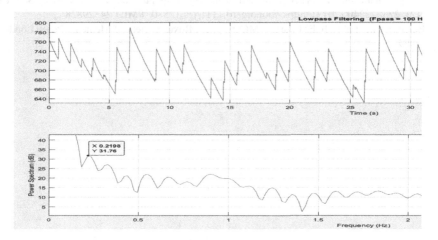

Fig. 5. Microwave Sensor results

7 Conclusion

The Smart device is designed to save children lives and make parents aware of the possible dangerous situations. The system is designed with a minimum cost and designed to be portable. The system can be integrated in any car if it is going to be used for alert purposes only and it can be built into the car system to take more actions such as controlling the AC unit and rolling down the windows to save children trapped in heated cars.

References

1. Null, J., CCM: Heatstroke deaths of children in vehicles (2018)
2. Grundstein, A.J., et al.: Evaluating infant core temperature response in a hot car using a heat balance model. Forensic Sci. Med. Pathol. **11**(1), 13–19 (2015)
3. Vanos, J.K., et al.: Evaluating the impact of solar radiation on pediatric heat balance within enclosed, hot vehicles. Temperature **5**(3), 276–292 (2018)

4. Izadi, A., Ghatan, Z., Vahdat, B.V., Farzaneh, F.: Design and simulation of life detection system based on detection of the heart beat using doppler frequency. In: IEEE International Symposium on Signal Processing and Information Technology (2006)
5. Chen, K.-M., et al.: Microwave life-detection systems for searching human subjects under earthquake rubble or behind barrier. IEEE Trans. Biomed. Eng. **47**(1), 105–114 (2000)
6. Carbon Dioxide. Wisconsin Department of Health Services. https://www.dhs.wisconsin.gov/chemical/carbondioxide.htm
7. Size of Vehicle. United States Department of Energy. https://www.fueleconomy.gov/
8. Hallett, S., Ashurst, J.V.: Physiology. In: StatPearls [Internet]. StatPearls Publishing, Treasure Island (FL), January 2018. https://www.ncbi.nlm.nih.gov/books/NBK482502/. Tidal Volume. Accessed 2 Feb 2019
9. Rodríguez-Molinero, A., Narvaiza, L., Ruiz, J., Gálvez-Barrón, C.: Normal respiratory rate and peripheral blood oxygen saturation in the elderly population. J. Am. Geriatr. Soc. **61** (12), 2238–2240 (2013). https://doi.org/10.1111/jgs.12580. PMID 24329828
10. Beardsell, I., et al.: MCEM Part A: MCQs, p. 33. Royal Society of Medicine Press, London (2009)

Cloud-Based IoT Smart Parking System for Minimum Parking Delays on Campus

Nesreen Alsbou[1(✉)], Mohamed Afify[1], and Imad Ali[2]

[1] University of Central Oklahoma, Edmond, OK 73034, USA
nalsbou@uco.edu
[2] University of Oklahoma Health Science Center,
Oklahoma City, OK 73104, USA

Abstract. Growing cities always have parking challenges and they are in need for creative ideas to solve this issue and avoid the time wasted in searching for empty parking spots. To overcome the problem, this paper proposes a simple solution using a low-cost cloud-based system design. The design will be initially implemented on campus in one parking lot at the University of Central Oklahoma. The goal is to make the faculties and students life easier by guiding them to empty parking spots. The design of the proposed system is discussed in this paper and preliminary data are presented including the cost function. The system will guide the users through the web-based application.

Keywords: Smart parking · Internet of Things (IoT) · Mobility · Cloud · Platform · Cost function · UBIDOTS · Fermi-Dirac · OpenStreetMap · Active nodes

1 Introduction

Most people waste a large amount of their time searching for an empty parking spot on a daily basis. Based on [1] the average time spent looking for parking across the U.S. is 17 h a year. In [2] a research done by UCLA urban-planning professor Donald Shoup found the average time a driver spent looking for an empty parking spot was 3.3 min. Therefore, in a typical search for parking spot in urban areas a driver can spend on average anywhere between 3 to 14 min. To solve the problem of parking delays, different solutions for smart parking were proposed such as the ones in [3] and [4]. However, most smart parking solutions only considered metered parking, curb parking or cars with RFID tags. Today we live in a world with advanced technologies where most people have smart devices and/or new cars equipped with different kinds of sensors, GPS, wireless connectivity and many other features. We can make use of these advanced technologies to solve many problems such as the problem of delays in parking lots. The University of Central Oklahoma (UCO), as well as most of the colleges in the United States, shares the same problem when it comes to parking spots. The problem becomes even worse during special events such as homecoming, graduation and football games. In order for drivers to make quick decisions, they need to know which parking lots have available parking spots. If the drivers are able to receive

V. Issarny et al. (Eds.): ICIOT 2019, LNCS 11519, pp. 131–139, 2019.
https://doi.org/10.1007/978-3-030-23357-0_11

information about the exact locations of available parking spots, the traffic congestion will be reduced and the traffic flaw will be smoother around campus.

This paper outlines the design of a smart parking system and shows the process of allocating free parking spots and navigating the users directly to them. The proposed smart parking system is a cloud-based system connected to the web and a cell phone application. The embedded system will be operated by a Microcontroller to send the serial information to a Wi-Fi Module. The Embedded system will be operated by a master board that will take readings and analyze them to make appropriate decisions. The system will use different kinds of sensors and a feedback mechanism to minimize the errors. The system will be operated in a low power which will minimize the battery power supply exchange up to roughly 3 years. The system is operated using C++, Java and android studio programs. The system is using the IoT intelligence network systems to analyze data and give a feedback through the user applications using the UBIO-DOTS platform cloud. In this paper, the IoT system is integrated with the smart real-time traffic congestion estimation and clustering technique described in [5]. The OpenStreetMap is used to reach the shortest path through active nodes. We applied a study on the smart parking guidance algorithm by adding some events and processing them through the platform to make different decisions similar to the method explained in the smart parking guidance system in [6]. The same concept was integrated by adding similar events with the available parking spots. To estimate the parking spot occupancy in [7], they used the spatial distribution, joint distribution and temporal distribution. In our paper, a spatial random process considering different factors that affect the probability and distribution of occupancy is used and we integrated the Fermi-Dirac distribution in our system to decide how occupancy is distributed through time and distance. In this paper, we are introducing a smart parking system designed at a low cost and low voltage compared to the systems available in the market.

2   Smart Parking System Description

The smart parking system contains three systems, two hardware systems acting as slaves and one software system acting as a master. The master system is responsible for communicating the data between the systems and the cloud. The first slave system is an operational system equipped with sensors to detect the parking slot occupancy when a vehicle is parked on campus in the parking lot. The second system is an embedded system that collect data and show traffic regulation status on an outdoor LCD screen. The LCD screen is located at the entrance of the parking lot and it displays the number of available free spots in the parking lot and the direction of their location.

2.1   Hardware System I

The first hardware system is equipped with two microcontrollers for a low power consumption solution. The system contains an ARDUINO Nano which is connected to a Wi-Fi Module Intel Edison and a magnetic sensor with a low power of 1.62 V and 0.14 A. The Arduino uses the interrupt mode to save power, it wakes up when interrupted to perform the required operations and then goes back to sleep. The magnetic sensor uses the interrupt method to wake up the device using the interrupt service as well.

The Wi-Fi Module start operating after the magnetic sensor detect a vehicle in the parking spot. The parking spot is equipped also with an IR sensor to take another reading and confirm there is a vehicle indeed in the parking spot. After the confirmation, the Wi-Fi Module sends a message to the server indicating the spot is occupied. The server then deliver the message to the cloud platform as shown in Fig. 1.

Fig. 1. Smart vehicle detection system.

2.2 Hardware System II

The second hardware system is the main data collection and analysis center. The center receives the data from the server, analyzes it and displays the information to the users on an LCD. The system contains an MKR1000 WI-FI module that receives data and connects it to an LCD screen as shown in Fig. 2. The system is enhanced with summing algorithms of the active nodes to calculate the number of free spots at every intersection in the parking lot and show it on the outdoor LCD. Therefore, a driver with no web connection is able to see the LCD and find out the available spots in the parking lot and their exact location, on the right, on the left or just straight forward as shown in Fig. 3.

Fig. 2. Parking status outdoor LCD

Fig. 3. Number of free spots displayed on the LCD

3 System Hardware and Algorithms

The system main purpose is to save the time of the driver and make it easier for him to find a parking spot. Once the point of interest is identified by the driver, the system will find all available parking spots around the point of interest and will give the driver the choice to pick an available spot. The system will then guide the driver to that spot using the shortest path. The system is designed to process three main events, point of interest, shortest path and spots availability as shown in Fig. 4. Once the data is processed, it goes to the cloud event which will decide on the navigation path for the user and send it to the cloud server then it goes to the interactive cloud application. The user will be given the choice through the cloud application to choose the path and this will be feedback to the cloud event.

Fig. 4. Flowchart of the three events

3.1 Parking Spots Availability and Allocation

The main system that detects the spot occupancy was tested in three different locations on UCO campus parking lot with three coordinates that used to locate the system on google maps through the cloud platform. The system used an Arduino which has two operations, first detect the vehicle through the magnetic sensor which can operate from 1.6 V to 3.6 V and then it gives a pulse to the embedded system to operate on a full mode. As the vehicle approaches the magnetic sensor a distortion of the magnetic field occurs as explained in [8]. The 3-axis magnetic sensor fixed data shows the normal earth magnetic field at -23, -177, -532. The sensor was calibrated to set these raw data to zero. Figure 5 show a graph of the magnetic sensor data. It shows a distortion level between negative 10 mg and 40 mg around 0.004 s. Once the magnetic sensor detects the vehicle it sends a value to the Intel Edison to operate and take reading with the IR sensors which is used to measure the distance of the car ground clearance to decide whether a vehicle is parked or not. Therefore, the IR sensor will double check for any errors and make sure that there is a vehicle in the parking spot. The IR sensor GP2Y0A21YK0F is used because of its wide range of detection [9] as shown in Fig. 6. The range of 10–80 cm is ideal for detecting any car including stock cars with minimum ground clearance of 18.5 cm and maximum of 22.0 cm [10]. Many cars on campus are not stock suspension which means their owners did not decrease the height clearance or increased it. When the IR sensor detects a vehicle, it will send an integer of 1 and if it is a false reading it will send 0, it keeps updating every 10 s. Every integer value is uploaded to the server to be processed and considered when decisions are made.

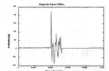

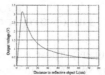

Fig. 5. Magnetic sensor vehicle detection   **Fig. 6.** IR Sensor range of detection, [9]

The IoT system is based on the API server, which is UBIDOTS, the server is analyzing the data in the platform, then it's sent to the Dashboard website and the Android app. Figure 7 shows the explained application layer, all these systems are integrated to send the data to the google maps that navigate the user to the parking spot, the analytics layer shows the data stored and then go to the data extraction and data analytics in the end. Last part is the network layer that has the Wi-Fi and the LTE that receive the data from the cloud.

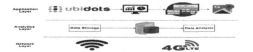

Fig. 7. IoT testing bed Layer

The two systems are operated through the HTTP requests of the cloud platform. The HTTP GET REUEST (HGR) is used to send the integer values to the cloud system as shown in Fig. 8. The data sent are between 0 and 1 to detect the spot occupancy.

Fig. 8. Cloud server for vehicle detection

The software event is set to communicate between the web application and the platform when a value of 1 is sent as it will POST an HTTP request through a third-party server to write a command to be posted on the google cloud platform to print a MARKER on the google map widget on the Web application. The software will send the value as context and status which will show a status on the marker that the spot is available. In case the integer sends a value of "1", the third-party server will operate an HTTP DELETE REQUEST which will delete the MARKER from the google map which means that the spot is not available anymore as shown in Fig. 9. An embedded HTML link for the real time google map is integrated and implemented into the android studio to generate an Android app that shows this on an online updated map. The user can go through the map in the app and choose any free parking spot available and shown by a Marker. Once the parking spot Marker is selected, the driver will be forwarded to the google maps app which will navigate the driver to the desired location as shown in Fig. 10.

Fig. 9. Google map of the free parking spots

Fig. 10. Android developed app for the smart parking system

The implemented IoT smart parking system has the capabilities to collect and display other related information such as weather status, live road conditions information and any warning messages from the Oklahoma department of transportation. All these information are displayed through the website application in addition to an integrated widget that has the total number of parking spots and the number of free spots available at any particular time as shown in Fig. 11.

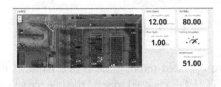

Fig. 11. Web application of the parking status

The second hardware system which is responsible for the live smart parking system information uses a software called WI-FI Get Client to get the values and save them in the firmware. An algorithm is developed and used to determine the exact location of the free parking spots and arrows displayed on the LCD are used to guide the users to the area in the parking lot with the free spots. The software is capable of detecting any issues with the smart parking system. For example, when the HTTP request is accepted it will send back a numerical value of "202" which means the request has been accepted for processing but if it receives any other value such as 4xx, then a bad request is detected. In this case, an error event is created and reported through a third-party server by sending an email to the company running the smart parking system and reporting the problem. The reported error message will include the specific device that caused the error, the exact location of the device in the parking lot, the issues were detected and possible solutions to the problem.

3.2   Smart Parking Case Study

A case study was performed on one of the University of Central Oklahoma parking lots shared between multiple buildings. Three of these buildings are considered as three points of interests for our smart parking system. The three buildings are the nursing building, the math building and the science building. Following a similar approach as in [7] we defined Eqs. 1, 2 and 3. In Eq. 1, the probability P is the occupancy of the targeted parking spot and P_1, P_2 *and* P_3 are the probability of parking occupancy close to the first building, second building and third building, respectively. Let $P_1P_2P_3$ be the probability of total occupancy in the parking lot shared by the three points of interest.

$$P = P_1 + P_2 + P_3 - P_1P_2P_3 \tag{1}$$

The probability of finding a parking spot during any time of the day including daily normal hours and special events can be calculated with respect to the distance by using a modified Fermi-Dirac formula. We can identify a relationship between the parking lot occupancy and the targeted parking spot by replacing the energy parameter in the Fermi-Dirac model with a distance parameter, d and considering the parameter KT as the effect factor on the steepness of the slope. Equation (2) shows the modified Fermi-Dirac model.

$$P(d) = \frac{1}{e^{\frac{d-p}{KT}} + 1} \tag{2}$$

Figure 12 shows the relationship between the parking lot occupancy and the distance to each of the points of interest. As expected, since the points of interest shared between multiple buildings, the probability of occupancy increases, as we get closer to the targeted parking spot. The intersection of the three curves in Fig. 13 will be the ideal target parking spot located at exactly the same distance from all three points of interest. The targeted parking spot is located at a distance of 20 m with a 50% probability of occupancy. The probability of occupancy with relation to the distance and time $P(d,t)$ can be found by multiplying the probability of distance P(d) by the probability of time P(t) as shown in Eq. 3.

$$P(d,t) = P(d) * P(t) \tag{3}$$

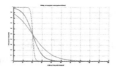

Fig. 12. Fermi – Dirac distribution of the point of interest.

3.3 Shortest Path to the Point of Interest Using Active Maps

After the driver determines the point of interest within the available parking spots, the system will navigate the user to that spot using the shortest path available after obtaining the coordinates of the driver and the coordinates of the point of interest. The system will use OpenStreetMap MATLAB function [11]. In our case study we exported a map of the University of Central Oklahoma as shown in Fig. 13 and the OSM version of the same boundary. We used the OpenStreetMap functions to plot the map streets and nodes as shown in Fig. 14 then we added it in parallel with the original PNG version as shown in Fig. 15. We plotted a figure of the active nodes on the map of each street intersection; we got a total of 883 ways and 3139 nodes as shown in Fig. 16. We plotted the active nodes on our map as shown in Fig. 17 to locate the shortest path between the nodes to navigate the driver through the ways in the map and guide him to his chosen spot. The smart parking system was tested successfully and displayed the shorted path between two nodes as shown in Fig. 18 were one node was chosen as a starting node (node 51) and another node was chosen as a target node (node 151).

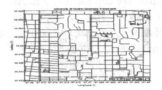

Fig. 13. University of Central Oklahoma (UCO) map

Fig. 14. MATLAB traced path of UCO campus area

Fig. 15. MATLAB traced path parallel to the image

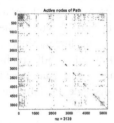

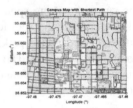

Fig. 16. Map active nodes

Fig. 17. Campus map with the active nodes

Fig. 18. Shortest path from node 51 to 151

4   Results and Future Work

This paper provides a simple IoT solution for the parking problem on campus. The solution utilizes smart devices and the cloud. The system included an application which was designed and created with an APK file using the Android studio to create a Cell Phone Application, A Token and Device ID were used to communicate between each device in the parking spot with the cloud through a packets of secure HTTP requests with the SSL Encryption which creates a secure encrypted connection between the server and the device. A formula is used to show the relation between the parking occupancy and the points of interest. The smart parking system was tested successfully, and the system was able to take a google map and generate an active node map and then identify the shortest path between two target nodes. In a future work, the goal is to have a complete smart system that control the entire campus. Cameras can be integrated on the side roads of the campus and give predictions of the traffic flow in and out of the campus and predict how many spot will be filled at any instant of time. RFID machine readers can be used too to collect data from the university tags to count the vehicles entering the university campus.

5   Conclusion

In this paper, a smart parking solution using the cloud is proposed to minimize parking delays for students, staff and faculty. The proposed system proved to be initially working successfully in achieving this goal considering cars that are both equipped with smart devices and unequipped. This proposed smart parking system is inexpensive and could provide a simple and cheap solution to the parking delay problem. The reduction in the cost is due to the use of the cloud and the app which guide the users to the closest available parking spot locations using smart devices they most likely have thus saving them time and money.

References

1. INRIX: INRIX Parking: a complete parking experience. inrix.com/products/inrix-parking/
2. Shoup, D.C.: Cruising for parking. Transp. Policy **13**(6), 479–486 (2006)
3. Pham, T.N., Tsai, M.-F., Nguyen, D.B., Dow, C.-R., Deng, D.-J.: A cloud-based smart-parking system based on internet-of-things technologies. IEEE Access **3**, 1581–1591 (2015)
4. Bandara, H.M.A.P.K., Jayalath, J.D.C., Rodrigo, A.R.S.P., Bandaranayake, A.U., Maraikar, Z., Ragel, R.G.: Smart campus phase one: smart parking sensor network. In: Manufacturing & Industrial Engineering Symposium (MIES) (2016)
5. Pattanaik, V., et al.: Smart real-time traffic congestion estimation and clustering technique for urban vehicular roads. In: 2016 IEEE Region 10 Conference (TENCON) (2016). https://doi.org/10.1109/tencon.2016.7848689
6. Shin, J.-H., Jun, H.-B.: A study on smart parking guidance algorithm. Transp. Res. Part C: Emerg. Technol. **44**, 299–317 (2014). https://doi.org/10.1016/j.trc.2014.04.010
7. Landry, D.M.W., Morin, M.R.: Estimating parking spot occupancy
8. Bugdol, M., Sgiet, Z., Krecichwost, M.: Vehicular detection system using magnetic sensors **9**(1) (2014)
9. SHARP: Distance Measuring Sensor Unit Measuring distance/Mouser Electronics. GP2Y0A21YK0F datasheet, November 2002
10. Gagan, M.: Cars with Best Ground Clearance in Hatch. SUV Segment, Sedan (2017)
11. Filippidis, I.: OpenStreetMap MATLAB Function, 15 November 2016

Correction to: Smart IoT In-Car Life Detector System to Prevent Car Deaths

Nesreen Alsbou, Ka Hei Samuel Chan, and Mohamed Afify

Correction to:
Chapter "Smart IoT In-Car Life Detector System
to Prevent Car Deaths" in: V. Issarny et al. (Eds.):
Internet of Things – ICIOT 2019, **LNCS 11519,**
https://doi.org/10.1007/978-3-030-23357-0_10

The original version of this chapter was revised. The surname of one of the authors inadvertently contained a typo. The surname has been corrected to "Chan".

The updated version of this chapter can be found at
https://doi.org/10.1007/978-3-030-23357-0_10

Author Index

Printed in the United States
By Bookmasters